HUMAN LIFE IS SACRED

Pastoral Letter
of the Archbishops and Bishops of Ireland
to the clergy, religious and faithful.

*Complete text
with introduction
and study guidelines*

Veritas Publications Dublin 1975
St. Paul Editions 1977

First published May 1975.
Designed by Steven Hope, LSIA.
Printed by John English and Co., Ltd., Wexford

Photo credits:
  Daniel Mastro, Jr.—cover
  HDC St. Louis — 21
  Monaghan — 13
  Society of St. Paul/Paul R. Schell — 41

This is the full text of the Pastoral Letter of the Irish Bishops, *Human Life is Sacred*, presented in one volume with an introduction and simple study guidelines.

The text was first published as four separate booklets, which sold 76,000 copies each and caused considerable interest and comment both in Ireland and overseas. The text was reproduced in the English language edition of *Osservatore Romano*, and permission has been granted for a special edition for the Philippines.

This edition is reprinted with the kind permission of the Irish Bishops' Conference, by Daughters of St. Paul, 50 St. Paul's Ave., Jamaica Plain, Boston, Ma. 02130, U.S.A.

Introduction

This pastoral letter deals with one of the main topics of our time. People have always discussed sex, marriage, human dignity and violence but never as openly and as continuously as now. Faced with this non-stop public debate the Christian may wonder what his religion has to offer. It is hoped that a careful reading of the pastoral will show the wealth of Christian teaching on human life.

The title is important: *Human Life is Sacred*. It means that life comes from God. Since Christ is God-made-man his life is the model of worthwhile human living.

What subjects are discussed? Parts One and Two talk about *Life*, Parts Three and Four deal with *Love*. Part One (*Yes to Life*) gives the Christian teaching on the rights of the unborn child; housing; education and family welfare. Part Two (*Thou Shalt Not Kill*) is about euthanasia; the care of the old and the dying; pain-killing drugs and violence.

The theme of love is carried through Parts Three and Four. Especially interesting is the section on the problems facing Irish marriages today. Many young people are puzzled by celibacy. They should read paragraph 89. The final part (*Love Gives Life*) is mainly about parenthood; children; and a restatement of the Catholic teaching on birth regulation.

Some discussion points have been added. They are meant to keep discussions centred on the text of the letter, to deepen knowledge of what it contains. This is not to discourage wider research and discussion, but knowing what is in the pastoral is a necessary first step.

Contents

Part One
YES TO LIFE

Respect for Life

1.   Human life is sacred, even before it is born. Sexuality and sexual love are sacred, as the mysterious source of human life. These truths have been honoured by the great majority of men all through history, whatever their religion and whatever their culture.

2.   Christians in particular have, until recently, been unanimous and undivided in their absolute respect for unborn life and in their view of what reverence for sex, the source of life, implies. These values have begun to be questioned only in recent years. It is necessary for us all to examine these matters again in the light of the Gospel and in the light of Christian and human conscience.

3.   It is our Christian faith which provides our deepest insight into the mystery of life and the surest guidance as to how life is to be respected. The Church has centuries of experience in dealing with men in all cultures and in all conditions. All this wise experience lies behind her judgments on human living. But her faith is much more than merely human insight: it is a sharing in the mind of Christ. St. Paul says:

> We teach, not in the way in which philosophy is taught, but in the way that the Spirit teaches us, showing how spiritual truths make spiritual sense . . . we are those who have the mind of Christ (1 *Corinthians* 2: 13-16).

The teaching of the Church, guided by the Holy Spirit of Christ, gradually forms in us "the same mind which was also in Christ Jesus" (*Philippians* 2: 5). We have, therefore, an obligation to form our beliefs and consciences in the full light of the teaching of the Church. This Pastoral Letter has been written in order to set out the teaching of the Church in the matter of human life and its origins in marriage.

The Value of Life

4. The Christian principle of respect for human life at every stage of its existence is firm and clear. God alone is the Lord of life. Man is made in his image and likeness. We come from God. We go to God. We belong to God. In the Psalms we read:

> Know that he, the Lord, is God.
> He made us, we belong to him (*Psalm* 99: 3).

> For it was you who created my being,
> knit me together in my mother's womb.
> I thank you for the wonder of my being (*Psalm* 138: 13-14).

God's commandment, "Thou shalt not kill," unconditionally forbids all taking of innocent human life from its beginnings in the womb until the end that God, not man, has set for it. One must have absolute respect for human life as coming from God's hands at the very first moment of conception and as remaining under God's care on earth until he takes it back to himself again in death.

5. Some will argue that not every life is of equal value. But in the eyes of God every life is of equal and of priceless value. We must see every life as having the value which it has for God. Christ speaks of the loving concern for each one of us which God has as our most dear Father:

> Can you not buy two sparrows for a penny? And yet not one falls to the ground without your Father knowing. Why, every hair on your head has been counted. So there is no need to be afraid; you are worth more than hundreds of sparrows (*Matthew* 10: 29-31).

Each human being is called to live with God forever. Each human being is one of whom Christ thought so much that he died for him. Here is where each human being gets his value. Some people have answered the question, "What is that man worth?", by stating the value of his assets or the amount of his annual earnings. The true answer is: "That man is worth the life's blood of Christ." There and only there is the true standard for judging the value of life.

6. Secular society has different priorities in its attitudes and laws. In many countries State law has come to allow abortion for a variety of reasons. The changes in the law which brought this about would not have been introduced unless public opinion had first been lulled by propaganda; but when changes of this kind in the law are introduced they change public opinion still further and much more rapidly in the same direction. Abortion is now discussed in many countries almost as if it raised no moral problem at all. People talk now instead as if the only problem were to find ways of making abortion still more widely available, faster and cheaper.

7. In this Letter, we are speaking primarily on the basis of our faith in Christ. We are speaking primarily to those who share that faith. But we confidently appeal also to the "unwritten laws" of the Creator, which can be seen by human reason to be written in God's creation and to be engraved in the heart of man, in his conscience and his sense of personal responsibility. During the whole of its history until very recently, and even before Christianity, the ethics of the medical profession found its cherished expression in the Hippocratic Oath. By the terms of this Oath, already five hundred years before Christ, doctors solemnly swore:

> I shall never, no matter who may demand it, supply a homicidal drug . . . I shall never supply any woman with an abortive pessary. By chastity and sanctity, I shall protect my life and my profession.[1]

A more modern form of this Oath, the Geneva Medical Oath, drawn up in 1948 by the World Health Organisation, says:

I shall keep absolute respect for human life, from the moment of conception.[2]

We are therefore at one with the oldest and noblest traditions of the medical profession when we take our stand for the sacred character and the absolute rights of unborn life. We are also at one with the deepest convictions of the human conscience.

8. When the Church states her moral principles, however, she appeals ultimately to the truth and love which Christ brought into the world. She takes the Divine Teacher as her model. She endeavours to speak clearly and without compromise; but she speaks with love for the human person, with respect for human intellect and for human freedom; and she speaks with the confidence that the inner force of the Christian message will, by God's grace, and because of its sheer truth and rightness, find an answering echo in the heart of man.

Abortion is Killing the Innocent

9. God's commandment, as we have seen, is that no human being may deliberately take away innocent human life. What life could be more innocent than that of the unborn child? Deliberate abortion is therefore always gravely sinful. The embryo or fetus possesses its fundamental right to life from the moment of conception. From that moment the fetus is already provided with all the genetic elements which will shape its future development as an adult human person. To use the language of genetics, the embryo, from the instant of the meeting of the mother and father cells, is already equipped with the entire "programme" of its future physical characteristics, right down to the minutest detail (including its unique and identifying finger-prints), as well as of its basic mental capacity and personality traits. Everything that education and environment will later have to work on is

already present in the embryo. Each single embryo, even though so small as to be invisible to the naked eye, is unique and un-repeatable. Strictly speaking, so far as in-built potential for future development is concerned, the newly-fertilised mother-cell has the same potential as the newly-born baby. A distinguished Professor of Midwifery has said:

> This is more than a potential human being; it *is* already a human being with potential, complete with every genetic detail, unique, individual and unrepeatable.[3]

From the day of conception to the day of birth, life in the womb is a continuing process of inter-locking events. To interrupt the process is to take innocent human life.

10. How could women and girls ever think of having an abortion performed if they realised the wonder and the beauty of the tiny being that is living and growing close to their heart? How can men be so heartlessly insensitive to the deepest feelings of women, so blind to the mysteries of parenthood, as to pressurise their partners into seeking abortions? Once their child is conceived, they are not about to become parents: they have become parents already. Any mother who has had the sorrow of a miscarriage knows that it was a baby that she lost.

11. The likeness of the parents is already stamped on the little being from the beginning. The human organs and features develop with astonishing rapidity. Before the first month is out, head and brain-cells, mouth and eyes are there. By the end of the fourth week, the beating of the heart has been detected. In the sixth or seventh week, the fetus will respond to a touch. Many abortions take place at twelve weeks. By then the baby has well developed features and its heart-beat can be easily identified. Two hearts are then beating together in the mother's body; but the small heart depends entirely on the large one, not only for the blood supply which brings it nourishment, but even more for the love which will allow it to develop its full human potential.

12.   Any form of abortion, however early it is performed and by whatever expert, is so crude and brutal as hardly to bear description. One method is for the little body to be "scraped out," that is to say cut up within the womb and pulled out in pieces with a forceps. Alternatively and more often the body is "sucked out" in parts by vacuum extraction. A third method — though this one tends to be avoided now as carrying risk to the mother — was to replace the fluid in which the baby lives by a salt or glucose solution; this burned up the fetus or killed it slowly by poisoning, and it was born dead some time afterwards by a false labour. At later stages of the pregnancy, the baby is removed from the mother by a surgical operation.   When lifted out of its home in the mother's womb, it is still alive.   After a while it dies of exposure.   People speak of a non-viable baby (one which cannot live outside the womb) as being not yet human. Let us not forget that any one of us would be non-viable if unable to walk and left out for long enough without clothing in the snow.

13.   It is not pleasant to speak of these matters. The facts of abortion are ugly. But they are the facts. It is dishonest to conceal them, or to speak of them in impersonal clinical phrases like "termination of pregnancy," "scraping the uterine lining," "emptying the uterus," and so on. Smooth words will not change evil things into good. Killing a baby is still killing a baby even if people call it "termination of pregnancy," or, more smoothly still, "deconception". For a man to kill his next-door neighbour is still murder, even if the man says he is only "terminating the occupancy of the adjoining residence."

14.   Abortion does not become in any degree less ugly or less evil if some State law permits it or if it is done in a public hospital by a specialist under a government health service. Mothers who consent to have this done have usually not been allowed to know, or have not permitted themselves to

think, about what it is that is being done to their baby. At seminars and discussions promoting abortion, lecturers impress upon nursing personnel that mothers are never in any circumstances to be told what the operation involves, and that the word "baby" is strictly never to be used in their hearing. It is to be replaced by such impersonal terms as "fetal parts," "fetal tissue", "contents of the uterus", etc. In this same connection, it is significant that research in America has found a high incidence of anxiety and guilt-feeling among para-medical personnel involved in abortions. This is true particularly among nurses. The occurrence of anxiety and guilt-feelings is related to the closeness of involvement in the actual abortion operation. One report states :

> The effect of actual observation and participation in the abortion procedure appears to be a powerful determinant in activating anxiety-producing psychological processes.

This report goes on to recommend that social workers involved in abortion work be so trained that they can help the other personnel involved to overcome their "negative emotional reactions". The technique recommended for doing this is to direct their attention away from the fetus, the operation and its result, and to divert it to the problems of the mother.[4]

15. It should be noted that the lobby which campaigned for legalised abortion in Britain planned their propaganda very carefully and selected their themes very skilfully. They made a deliberate decision to concentrate on the "hard cases". The campaign was led by a body called the Abortion Law Reform Association. Two of the members of this body wrote a book about their campaign. One of the things they say is this:

> There was (and still is) so much latent public distaste for the very idea of abortion that it was obvious throughout the Reform Campaign that they would only be able to carry the country with them if they concentrated on the hard cases.

The same two writers make a number of other revealing

statements. They point out that the Association made great play with opinion surveys. They admit that in the area of abortion "almost all figures were (and still are) subject to dispute"; but they go on to say that the organisers of the campaign discovered that opinion surveys were, as they very candidly put it, a "match-winning tactic". Another success-ful tactic, they report, was to involve the women's organisa-tions in the movement. Every move depended, of course, on the help of the media, and this was willingly forthcoming. Our two authors record with delight that "the mass-circulation newspapers realised that abortion was a popular subject", and that from the moment this realisation dawned, "every event was eagerly gobbled up and disgorged by press, radio and television". Finally, and this was the most import-ant point of all, the Association worked hard and successfully at, as they put it, "lining up friends at the centre of power". It is useful to bear in mind these hints from inside the move-ment about how a successful lobby in the area of public morality is worked.[5]

Rights of the Unborn

16. People who support abortion speak as if the unborn baby had no rights. Yet, if a father dies before his child is born, regardless of what the stage of the pregnancy, the child when born has legal rights of inheritance. In the case of the thalidomide babies, babies injured between the time of conception and birth were found entitled to compensation. Recently the English Law Commission recommended that compensation be claimable for unborn babies injured in the womb by the fault of another. The United Nations Organisation in 1959 declared:

> The child, because of its physical and mental immaturity, needs special care and safeguards, including legal safe-guards, before as well as after birth.[6]

Considerable embarrassment is caused to legal people by the

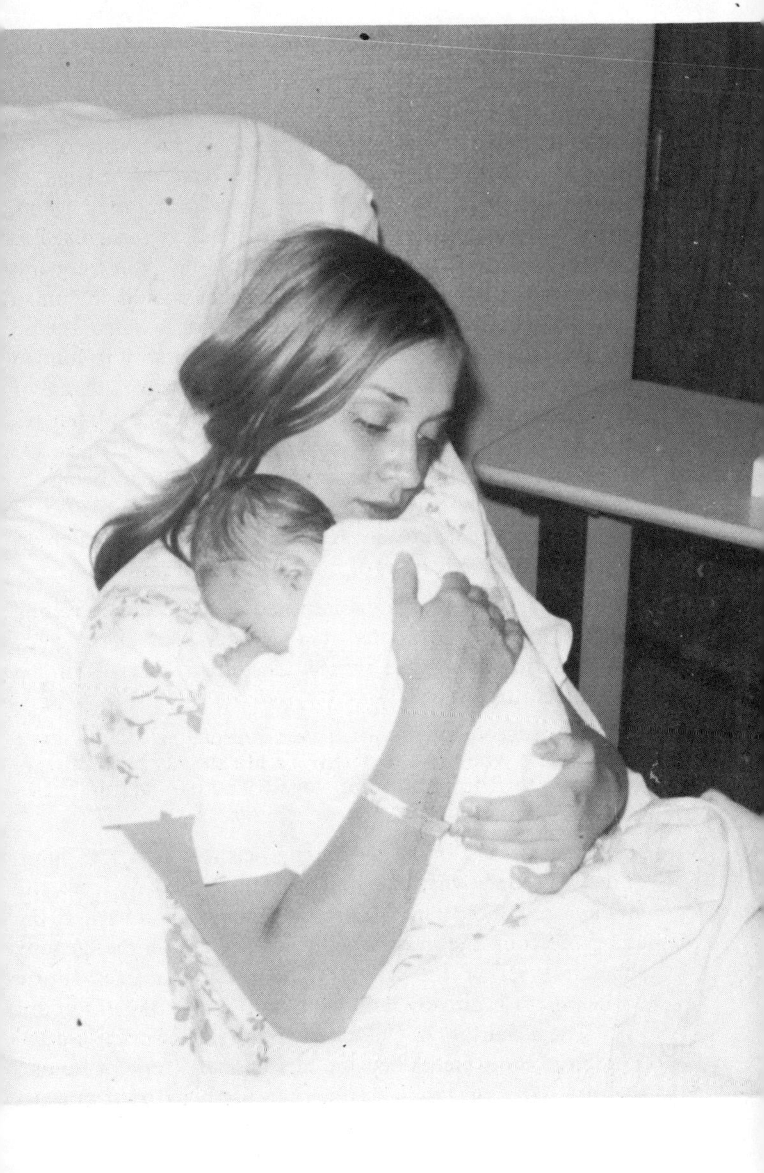

effort to reconcile these facts with the law permitting the killing of unborn babies.

17. Recently some philosophers and theologians have argued that the person becomes a person only when recognised as such by the community. They call this an act of "humanisation". To refuse birth to a child, they claim, simply means that it is not being accepted or recognised as a person, and that therefore it is not a person. But the point is that we are not free to refuse to recognise another human being as a person. Refusal to recognise another human being as a person is in fact the essence of all immorality in human relations. It is the basis of all oppression, torture, denial of civil rights, religious and racial discrimination, exploitation, all forms of inhumanity of man to man. All of these are simply ways of refusing to recognise other human beings as human. Once human life exists, we are *morally bound* to respect its right to life, to development, to human dignity. Otherwise, the very basis of morality is undermined.

18. The earliest Christian writers had no hesitation in calling abortion murder, no matter at what stage of the pregnancy it was performed. One writer, Tertullian, already in the second century, said:

> To prevent birth is anticipated murder; it makes little difference whether one destroys a life already born or does away with it in its nascent stage. The one who is to become a man is already a man.[7]

19. In any case, modern genetic science makes it more difficult to deny that the human soul is present from the moment of conception. As we have pointed out earlier, the embryo, from the first instant, possesses all the genetic characteristics of the adult. The programme for future development is already laid down on the first day of unborn life. The adventure of every human life begins in the womb. The fetus could never become human if it were not human already. The view which is most in harmony with modern

science is that the spiritual soul is present from the first moment of conception.

Consequences of Abortion

20. When discussing abortion in the past, people used to speak of the cruel dilemma of 'choice' between the life of the mother, which could be endangered by the continuance of the pregnancy, and the life of her unborn child. Such cases were always extremely few in number. We thank God that nowadays, where modern obstetric facilities are available, such cases are almost non-existent. It is strange that the pressure for abortion should have come principally from those countries where medical science is most advanced; for in fact advances in medicine and progress in ante-natal and obstetric services had eliminated most of the cases in which pregnancy could be a danger to the life of the mother.

21. The statistics from countries which have legalised abortion are revealing in this regard. The "indications" for which abortion is sought and obtained are for the most part of a psychological, social or economic kind, rather than based on grounds of physical danger or disease. Figures for England show that the "life or death" situation applied to only a tiny fraction of the total number of abortions. Taken together, all cases that could for any reason, whether medical or psychological, be really called "hard cases", account for not more than 2 per cent of all the registered abortions carried out in England in recent years.[8]

22. Some abortions are now performed on the grounds of the likelihood of the child's being born defective or handicapped. This, however, even if it could be demonstrated with certainty, would still not justify the deliberate killing of the innocent. It may be hard to see the meaning of a handicapped child's life, and hard for parents to accept it, if they do not look at life on earth with the eyes of faith. But if we

judge life and its worth by the standards of physical health and worldly welfare alone, then we have quite simply turned our backs upon the Gospel of Christ. In any case, those who have not experienced it will never know the amount of consolation that has been brought to parents in reward for the stress of caring for their handicapped child. The capacity for affection of many of these children is the joy of their parents' hearts. History will never calculate the amount of good that has been brought into our world by the devotion of parents and the care of the wider community in coping with the problems of handicapped children. Great progress has been made recently in social attitudes to this problem and in social provision for it. Great advances have been made in the education of children suffering from all forms of handicap. This is one outstanding example of how society can uplift itself by accepting and coping with suffering. Abortion, on the other hand, is a striking instance of how society can degrade and perhaps destroy itself by systematic refusal of suffering.

23. Abortion does not even succeed in eliminating suffering. It has to be remembered that God has provided in the mother's body quite remarkable systems of security and protection for the unborn child during all the stages of the pregnancy. Interference with these systems can be injurious to the mother as well as fatal to the child. These systems include instincts deeply embedded in the mother's personality. Abortion, by violating these womanly instincts, can lead in the long run to psychological disturbance to the mother. Some researchers have reported a notable proportion of mothers who suffer emotional disturbance after the abortion. Many suffer, in one degree or another, from guilt-feelings. There is a tendency, in much of the discussion about abortion, to ignore such findings. They are likely to be verified particularly, of course, in countries of Christian and especially Catholic background; but similar reports have come from non-Christian countries like Japan.

It should be noted too that a high proportion of legal abortions are sanctioned for psychiatric reasons; but it is known that those mothers who are severely emotionally disturbed by a pregnancy are precisely the ones who are more likely to be disturbed by post-abortion doubts and guilt-feelings. Research also suggests that some harmful physical effects for the mother herself and some risks for her future pregnancies can be traced to abortion.[9]

Legalisation Increases Demand

24. Since the Abortion Act came into force in Britain in 1967, the number of abortions notified has risen steadily year by year, going from 25,000 in 1968 to 170,000 in 1973. The figures speak for themselves. As the law stands at present, the situation seems to come very close to abortion on demand. And all this, it should be noted, is happening in a country where there is widespread availability and use of contraceptives. The two pro-abortion writers whom we quoted earlier point out that

> the problem (of unwanted children) is actually getting worse, despite the universal availability of contraceptives.

They argue:

> Abortion on request is a logical concomitant of contraception on demand.[10]

Availability of contraception will not lessen recourse to abortion: it will only spread still further the mentality and style of life which produce the demand for abortion. There are no easy options to take the place of moral living.

25. Some people sincerely believed that a legal measure of control would at least reduce the number of criminal abortions, with all the appalling risks and problems which these are causing. There are indications, however, that criminal abortions are continuing, side by side with the legal abortions. This has also been the experience in other countries with a longer history than Britain of legalised abortion. Further-

more, abusive practices operating under the actual cover of the law have often gone far to remove the distinction between criminal and legal abortions.

26. A responsible society would surely find other ways of coping with the problem of criminal abortions than simply to try to introduce legal abortion. Protection for unborn life should be part of society's whole commitment to the improvement of the quality of human life. There is a strange contrast in modern society between the genuine compassion which lies behind movements to abolish capital punishment and to reform the whole penal code for offenders, on the one hand, and, on the other, the barbarous killing of unborn babies. Indeed, the more one thinks of the terrible crime which abortion is, the more one finds that it is in complete contradiction with everything that a caring and compassionate society wishes to be. Modern society sincerely wishes and tries to be caring and compassionate. How can one explain the contradiction? One seems forced to the conclusion that sexual freedom has become such an obsession with modern society that it will sacrifice anything, even unborn babies, to appease this new absolute.

"Yes" to Life

27. The Constitution *On the Church in the Modern World* of Vatican II declared:

> God has conferred on man the surpassing ministry of safeguarding life, a ministry which must be fulfilled in a manner worthy of man. Therefore, from the moment of conception, life must be guarded with the greatest care — abortion and infanticide are unspeakable crimes.[11]

28. But we should not just say that the Church is "against abortion". We should say that the Church is *for* life. The Church says "Yes" to life. The Church has been saying "Yes" to unborn life, without any hesitation or reservation, for two thousand years. In recent years, since the abortion

debate became a public issue in country after country, nearly every Catholic Hierarchy in Europe, in America and everywhere the issue has been raised, has responded by once more clearly and strongly and unanimously repeating this great "Yes" to unborn life.

29. In Ireland, we are far from being unaffected by the problem and by the accompanying discussion. Experience elsewhere, as we have already indicated, shows only too clearly what carefully organised pressure-groups can do to confuse and then to change public opinion. More immediately disturbing is the fact that considerable numbers of Irish girls are already going to England each year to have abortions performed. At present more than 2,200 Irish girls are officially registered as having abortions in Britain each year. More than half of these are from the Republic. Since the introduction of legal abortion, probably at least 8,000 Irish-resident girls and women have had abortions under the British Act. Over half of these are from the Republic. This clearly could not be happening without encouragement and advice from people they consult in this country. Those who advise or arrange abortions for girls and women who consult them bear as great, if not a greater degree of guilt than the girls and women themselves. These figures indicate widespread moral confusion and lack of knowledge. This is the context in which we write this Letter.

30. As we write it, we are aware of the agonies of conscience and the tortures of remorse which many girls who have had abortions are now suffering. We want to speak to them too. We want to assure them of the boundless compassion and unlimited mercy of Christ. He loves them. He loves to forgive. He has told us that he has more joy in forgiving sinners than he receives from the just who do not think they need forgiveness. No-one is excluded from his love. No matter what the past, he offers everyone forgiveness and peace. His "Yes" to life is also an unconditional "Yes" to all who come in sorrow and love to ask his pardon.

The Quality of Life

31. The Church says "Yes", not just to human existence, but to the quality and dignity of human life. The Christian demand is that all human life should be permitted and enabled to develop to the full dignity and quality of living which befit a human person and child of God. Nothing less than that is what is commanded by Christ's command to love our neighbour as we love our own self. The Christian "Yes" to life includes a call for freedom, for adequate education, for proper living conditions, for more just distribution of wealth and opportunity, for protection of the human environment, and for more responsible use of the resources of nature. The Church is not simply "against abortion"; she is *for* life and *for* man and *for* human dignity and social justice.

32. It is often said nowadays that we should not consider so much the mere existence of life, but rather the quality which that life has the prospect of attaining. Some argue that unless unborn life can be assured of a certain quality, then the mere fact of its existence is deprived of value. Or that if the existence of unborn life seriously lessens the prospect of an acceptable quality of life for the mother or her family, then the unborn life cannot be said to have a right to exist.

33. This argument turns moral principles upside down. Life has the right to quality and dignity because it exists. Life does not derive the right to exist from the quality which circumstances seem likely to give to it. Once human life exists, then those who conceived it have the obligation to respect its right to continue to exist. They have, at the same time, the obligation to create the conditions which will enable it to develop in a manner worthy of its human dignity. If parents cannot themselves ensure this, then society has the strict duty to come to their help with all the supports that are necessary to give this new life a quality corresponding to its sacred character as a human person, made in the image of God.

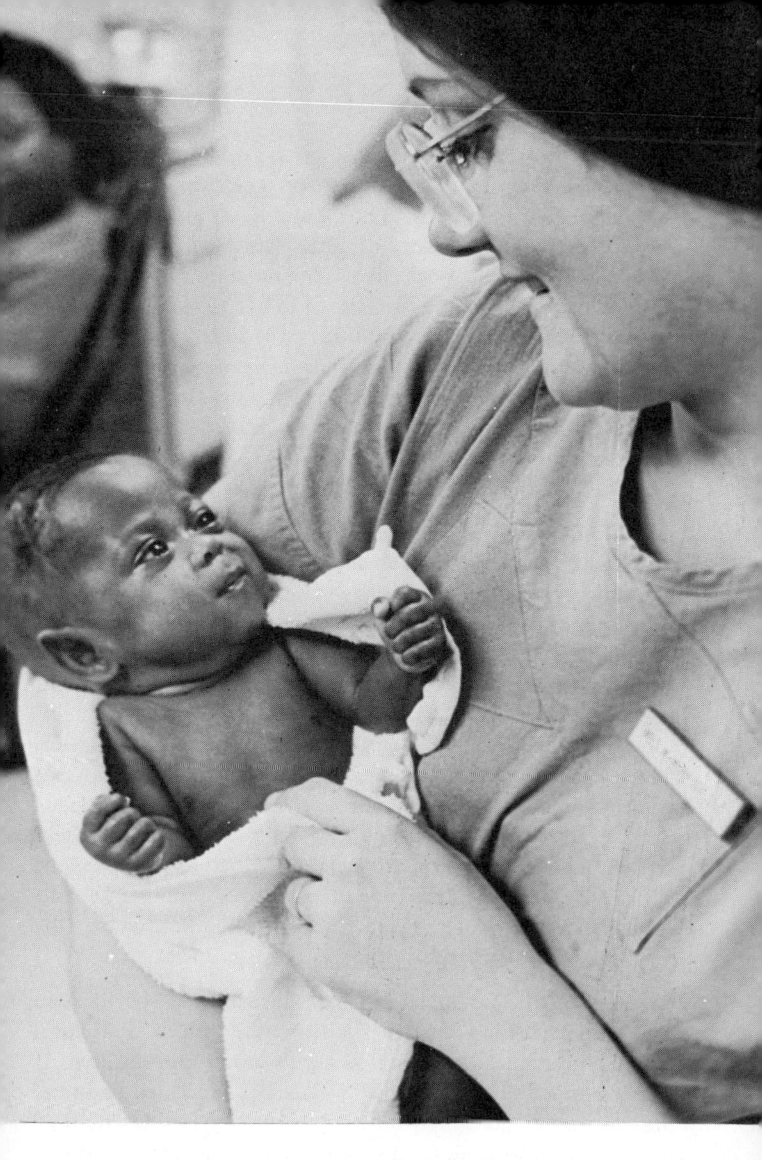

The Christian demand is that all human life should
be permitted and enabled to develop to the full
dignity and quality of living which befit a human
person and child of God.

Social Justice

34. It is not enough for the Christian community to lay down absolute moral principles and then feel that it has discharged its obligations. The Church must indeed proclaim the absoluteness of the law of God. But having proclaimed God's law, she must go further. She must do everything she can to ensure that people are helped to live up to the requirements of God's law. A moral principle must not be laid on men's backs like "a heavy and unsupportable burden", by someone who "will not move a finger" to help men to bear it (*cfr. Matthew* 23:4). To enunciate a moral principle is, at the same time, to be obliged to show compassion and to offer help to those on whom the principle may bear heavily.

35. While the Church rejects abortion, she also urges Christians to work to remedy and remove those circumstances which move people to have recourse to abortion. The very existence of unborn life creates an obligation on all concerned to respect that life. This obligation bears, in the first instance, on both the parents of that unborn life. But there will always be parents who cannot cope without society's help. Society has an obligation to come to their help. It is not enough to do this by noble declarations in the country's Constitution. Effective measures of family welfare and child-care are essential. Ireland still lags behind in many of these areas. There are secular societies which could put our Christian society to shame in the matter of family and child welfare. We are catching up gradually; but we must not be content with our pace of progress towards social justice.

36. One of the foremost duties of Christians in society is to work for conditions in which all the children of the nation will be guaranteed equality of dignity and opportunity. If circumstances do not promise to a newly conceived child the quality of life to which its human dignity entitles it, then society has a strict duty to seek to change the circumstances, not to extinguish the life. There could be no clearer instance

of the principle that society and its laws are made for men, not men for the convenience of society. Legalising abortion is society's easy way and lazy way and sinful way out of its responsibilities.

37. The Christian must continue to press upon society its duty to provide adequate housing at prices which are not a crippling burden upon families, and to provide proper family living conditions. Christians must continue to press for more funds for housing, especially for the less privileged sectors. Speculation in land for house building is often the unearned profit of a few at the expense of the most vital need of the many. There should be strict control of the prices of building land. In housing developments, Christians must strive to ensure that in every estate proper provision is made for recreational facilities and social amenities for families, and especially for children and mothers. Housing programmes which provide houses only, without such amenities, are a very short-lived and false economy. Many of the housing developments which we have had up to now have been simply creating conditions for youth maladjustment and social unrest in the future. They are social time-bombs with slow-burning fuses.

38. The Church is constantly extending and expanding marriage counselling services. No praise could be too great for the dedication with which so many priests, doctors and counsellors sacrifice their time and energy to enable couples to prepare responsibly for Christian marriage, as well as to assist them in the problems and difficulties of living it. The Church invites doctors, nurses and married people them-selves to acquire the knowledge needed to be able to impart instruction in the use of morally acceptable methods of birth regulation. Doctors have a special contribution to make. Many doctors are already doing magnificent work in these fields. There is work for many more doctors with similar motivation. Nurses too render indispensable service in

marriage counselling. All this work is bringing inestimable benefit to the health and well-being of society. It deserves more support from public funds. Public authority should make available to hard-pressed mothers the medical, psychiatric or material help which they need. It is particularly important that ante-natal counselling and care be available, that social and welfare services for expectant mothers be improved, and that modern obstetric facilities be put within the reach of the entire population. It should go without saying that all such services should be in accord with the consciences of those expected to avail of them.

39. Parents with small children, and especially larger families, will be exposed to particularly painful stresses in the period of severe inflation through which we are now passing. Social justice requires that the consequent burdens be as equally shared as possible. We rejoice that budgetary planning is becoming more family-centred. We hope that future planning will continue to increase family allowances and provide more effective tax relief related to the number of children. It is only right that we should pay tribute to the immense benefits conferred on families and on the nation by the introduction of free post-primary education. It is, however, important that this great achievement should not be set at risk by failure to make its financing keep pace with inflation or to allocate finances fairly as between different types of schools. In many respects, our educational system still needs to be improved, particularly in the direction of making access to third level education more open to all income groups; yet immense progress has already been achieved.

Respect for Marriage

40. A Christian community must have high esteem for the sacramental grace of marriage and the sacredness of married

love. In modern society, there are strong pressures to separate love and sex from marriage; and Christians must resist these pressures. Christian teaching regarding the sinfulness of sexual intercourse outside of marriage has not changed and will not change. There can never be question, for the Christian, of equating sexual intercourse outside marriage with the sexual union which is sanctified by God's grace in the sacrament of marriage. It is criminal that men so often exploit the loneliness and insecurity of unmarried girls, and even the innocence and trustingness of very young girls. For every unmarried mother there is an unmarried father, often leading a double life, and keeping his "respectability" at the expense of his moral responsibility.

41. Our esteem for marriage must never lead us to adopt a harsh and rejecting attitude towards the unmarried mother. To the unmarried mother, Christians must always show the compassion, the kindness and the support which she and her child need. It is above all to her parents that she ought to be able to look for understanding and forgiveness. To show an unfeeling and unforgiving attitude in this situation is un-Christian and can have tragic consequences. Christ's own treatment of sinners gives the model of a truly Christian judgment. Christ's example shows that there is a complete distinction between the Christian attitude and the merely permissive one. It is relevant to recall that our Lord himself once was a baby for whom the world had no welcome and, on the point of death, his last human concern was that his mother should have a loving home. At this point, we pay tribute to the many religious and lay institutes which, for many years, have been showing a genuinely Christ-like love and welcome towards unmarried girls and their babies. The range of services available in this country for unmarried mothers is excellent. It is not sufficiently known. We say with confidence that any intending mother will receive in this country a quality of care and compassion equal to that to be found anywhere. There is no need to leave the country

for such services. This fact adds to the tragedy of having girls leave the country for abortions. It adds to the guilt of those in this country who advise or assist girls to go to Britain for abortions.

42. We regret, however, that, in the community at large, there has sometimes in the past been a lack of compassion for unmarried mothers and a lack of respect for their children. The way we have sometimes spoken of these children seemed to blame them for their birth. But they are just as innocent and as deserving of respect as other children, and they are no more responsible than other children for the faults of their parents. The children must always be surrounded with love, respect and support, both from their parents' families and from society. On the other hand, however, one must deplore and resist the tendency to glamourise the so-called "one parent family". Marriage and marriage alone is the true expression of love and the normal condition for the emotional security and maturity of children.

From God and to God

43. In Michelangelo's representation of the creation of man in the Sistine chapel, God is shown as reaching lovingly across infinity to draw man out of nothingness and attract him upwards to himself. The divine finger which creates is also a finger which beckons, calls, invites. Life is God's gift: it is also God's invitation. From the moment of conception, each human life is called back to the Father. No-one has the right to put an end to a life which God meant to grow into knowledge and love of himself and meant to share his life and love forever. It is to God that we must answer for what we do or allow to be done to the lives he has created, whether they are already born or are still in the womb.

44. This invitation of every human life to come to God derives from creation itself. It is renewed still more power-

Life is God's gift: it is also God's invitation.

fully by baptism. Baptism gives a child a share in the very relationship of Christ Himself with the Father; baptism calls the child to be with Christ forever in the love of the Father. St. Ignatius of Antioch, while awaiting martyrdom, wrote of hearing "a murmur of living water that whispered within him: Come to the Father". The water in question was the water of his baptism. Water, as we know, seeks its own level. The level of the water of baptism, it could be said, is the level of the eternal life of the Father. Baptism constantly raises us up to the life of heaven. St. Irenaeus said: "The glory of God is a living man"; — that is to say, man living with the human life he received at conception, man living with the Christ-life he received at baptism. It is only in the light of baptism, the eternal love which God gives to us in baptism and the eternal life to which he calls us through baptism, that we can realise the fuller dimensions of what is happening in the womb. The deepest questions of both faith in God and in his Christ and of the survival of man and of civilisation are at stake in the discussion regarding abortion. The Christian can have no other stand than the stand for life; for his faith is in One who came "so that they may have life and may have it to the full" (*John* 10: 10).

Part Two:
THOU SHALT NOT KILL

God Gives Life

45. When the Catholic Church speaks of reverence for human life, the words are meant to be taken in their widest sense. We do not isolate the defence of unborn life from the defence of human life and dignity in other areas where these are being cheapened, endangered or destroyed. In all these areas, the same principle applies: Innocent human life is inviolable; no man has the right to suppress it.

46. This principle derives immediately from the fact that God is the Creator of Life. He gives life and He takes it away; we live out our lives in the shadow of his providence. Each human destiny is a mystery whose source is hidden in God's eternal plan of love, and whose end no human eye can see, because it is destined to open out in the eternal vision of the living God. Each life is sacred because only God knows when it has run its course.

47. All this we could already know by reflection on human experience. But this knowledge is reinforced by our Christian faith. When faith in God declines, man's sense of the value of human life suffers. When reverent fear of God lessens, man's fear of the taking of human life declines also. There is a link between the two parts of the phrase — "He fears neither God nor man". Our Lord himself said that the first and greatest commandment was to love God; and that the second was to love one's neighbour as oneself; and he added that the second was like the first. It is God we honour when we reverence man. It is God we insult when we do violence to human life or human dignity.

Science and Life

48. Experience itself is enough to show that no man can be trusted with absolute power over the lives of others, and especially with absolute power over life and death. It is a grim fact that throughout history each new piece of scientific knowledge and of technological power has been used for war and destruction and for the enslavement of men, just as much as for increasing the sum of human happiness. Science alone will not save man. The only totally secure barrier for man against attacks upon his right to life is the absolute principle that innocent human life is sacred, and that every human being has its right to life directly from God, and not from any human authority. Because he saw this so clearly, Pope Pius XII taught:

> No man, no human authority, no science, no medical, eugenic, social, economic or moral indication can offer or produce a valid juridical title for disposing directly of innocent human life (*Address to Midwives*, 1951).

Euthanasia

49. The right to life is at stake at one end of the scale in abortion; at the other end of the scale in euthanasia. It may be thought that this question of euthanasia is not relevant to Ireland. But consider what happened in Britain. The delicate tip-toeing into the legalising of abortion has been succeeded, now that abortion has arrived on a grand scale, by an equally delicate tip-toeing into the field of euthanasia. We would be foolish indeed if we imagined that we in Ireland have some immunity from this kind of creeping paralysis of the moral sense.

50. "Euthanasia" is, of course, derived from two Greek words meaning "pleasant or painless death". This is one instance, among many in modern society, where a good motive is supposed to make wrong things right. A merciful

motive (preventing pain or hardship) is held to make right something which, in itself and in other circumstances, would be admitted to be wrong (putting an innocent person to death).

51. The advocates of euthanasia often begin by talking about a "right to die", a "right to choose death"; and insist, at least at first, that euthanasia should be a matter of voluntary choice. A suffering or old person should, it is claimed, have the right to ask for a death-dealing drug; or, since a person who is in extreme pain or senile would not be capable of a rational decision, he should, they argue, be allowed to draw up a previous declaration, asking in advance for euthanasia to be administered in specified circumstances; and the doctor should, they claim, be legally free to implement this decision when these circumstances arrive.

52. It is significant that the arguments advanced for euthanasia are exactly parallel to those advanced for abortion. It is argued that the fetus is human only potentially; that it is not a free or rational person; that it is kept alive only through the life-support given it by others. In exactly the same way, it is said that the incapacitated or senile person is only "a piece of human wreckage" (this is an exact quotation from a recent plea for euthanasia)[12]; that he is "only a vegetable"; that he is being kept alive only by the kindness of relatives and the life-support systems of medicine. It is, in fact, impossible to construct a definition of abortion in such a way as to justify abortion but to forbid euthanasia. Once society accepts legalized abortion, it becomes logically and morally impossible to oppose legalized euthanasia.

53. But the matter cannot stop even with voluntary euthanasia. It is obvious, and is admitted even by some euthanasiasts themselves, that an even stronger case can be made for euthanasia for people incapable of choice (such as mentally-handicapped or incurably mentally ill people) than can be made for so-called voluntary euthanasia. It is obvious that

the very same case can be made for killing mentally or physically handicapped infants after birth as can be made for killing them in the womb. But surely, with all this, we are in the world of Nazi Germany, not in that of Western liberal democracy. Liberal reformers are outraged at this comparison. But it is difficult to see how it can be avoided. The comparison is in fact resisted only by arguing that the motive and the intention are totally different. But this, in turn, is to hold that it is motive and intention which determine morality. If that were so, then racial discrimination would not be racial discrimination if it were intended for the ultimate good of the coloured people themselves; torture would not be torture if it were an effective means to combat terrorism; murder would not be murder if it were done in the interests of "my country" or "my cause".

54. What must always be remembered is that certain actions are good or evil in themselves already, apart from the motive or intention for which they are done. Deliberately to take one's own life is suicide and is gravely wrong in all circumstances. To co-operate with another in taking his own life is to share in the guilt of suicide. Deliberately to terminate the innocent life of another is murder, no matter how merciful the motives, no matter how seemingly desirable the result.

Death with Dignity

55. Advocates of euthanasia speak of "the right" to choose a dignified death instead of a degrading and disgusting twilight life. But dignity in old age and in pain are a matter of the spirit even more than of the body. Dying can be an opportunity — a man's last opportunity — for showing courage, nobility and serenity. A priest has written a book about dying: he calls it "*The Last Achievement*".[13] One has a right to die one's own death; but, for the Christian, his own death is the death willed for him by God, at the time he

Only God can say when one's years are completed
and one's course towards him is run. Life itself is
grace. The time of one's life is a time of God's love
and of God's grace. It is not for us to put limits to
his grace or his love.

wills and in the manner he wills. Only God can say when one's years are completed and one's course towards him is run. Life itself is grace. The time of one's life is a time of God's love and of God's grace. It is not for us to put limits to his grace or his love.

56. Dignity in old age and in pain are above all a matter of whether one knows that one is loved. No one who knows he is loved ever loses dignity. It is true that long illness and helplessness impose a great strain on the love of relatives. But if euthanasia existed as a possibility, the strain on love would become unbearable, both for the relatives and for the patient. The patient, the relatives, the doctor, could never have complete trust in one another. The patient might feel he was being selfish if he did not seek death in order to relieve relatives of the hopeless burden. He might feel unwanted and suspect that relatives were silently hoping he would ask for death. Both relatives and patient would be unsure of their doctor's attitude or of the purpose of his prescriptions. The chief problems and trials of the old and the fatally ill are a sense of total and helpless dependence on the goodwill, the patience and the love of others; insecurity; the suspicion of being unwanted; the fear of being resented as a burden or rejected. The possibility of euthanasia would increase the insecurity to the point of torment. Once the principle of euthanasia became accepted, there could be great temptation for health authorities to advocate or condone it, as a way of reducing pressure on the health services and freeing resources for other areas of medical care.

57. Those with experience of nursing the terminally ill and the old know that what they fear is not death so much as being abandoned and left alone. They fear being unloved and unwanted even more than they fear pain. Everything is bearable, even death loses terror, in the presence of those who love us. People with experience agree that a substantial component of all pain is psychological. Fear of pain, anti-

cipation of pain, anxious uncertainty about one's ability to bear pain, these greatly increase the pain itself. Every kind of pain is increased by insecurity and isolation or the fear of rejection. One very effective pain-lessening procedure is to inspire confidence in the patient by creating around him an atmosphere of security and trust. This depends chiefly on convincing the patient that one will be with him to the end and will not leave him alone at the end. Pain and senility are much more a test of the love and fidelity of relatives and friends than they are of the endurance of patients. It has been truly said that if a person asks for euthanasia, someone has failed him.

Care for the Dying

58. In a culture where euthanasia becomes thinkable Christians must commit themselves anew to the care of the old and dying. One student of the problem has written recently that:

> the answer to the problems currently facing us lies first and foremost in changing the attitude of society and not in changing the laws of the land.[14]

The new *Rite of Anointing and Pastoral Care of the Sick* offers great new opportunities. It is a reflection on the faith and charity of the whole Church community if any sick or dying person is allowed to feel that they suffer or die alone. Each suffering or dying Christian is, and should be able to feel himself to be, surrounded and supported by the prayer and care and ministry of healing of the Church.

59. All Christians have a share in the Church's ministry of healing. This is itself a continuation throughout time of Christ's own ministry of healing and companioning the suffering. Medical and nursing personnel, of course, side by side with priests, have a special place in this Christian ministry of healing. Doctors, despite the pressures and harassments of modern medical practice, should be inspired by the

honourable traditions of their profession to seek to continue to be "family doctors", ministering to persons, not just cases, and showing an undiminished interest in patients even when there is no more hope of cure. More doctors and nurses should be encouraged to include geriatrics and terminal care among their specialisations. There is now available an almost unlimited variety of analgesic drugs and interventions; and skilful use of these can ensure that no pain need be totally unbearable.

60. As we have said earlier about abortion, euthanasia is society's lazy way and unloving way of getting rid of the problem of pain and old age. The author we quoted earlier concludes his article by saying:

> I firmly believe that a positive approach to death by society in general, together with compassionate, competent medical care and considerate, patient-orientated nursing hold the answer to our present problem.[15]

A Happy Death

61. The real answer to the euthanasia mentality is for Christians to witness, both in personal conviction and in words, but above all by example, to the faith which gives us the joyful hope that "death is swallowed up in victory" (1 *Corinthians* 15:55). When the Christian speaks of a happy death he is speaking of something much more than a death without pain. For him death has positive meaning as the door opening on new life. In his resurrection Christ deprived death of its power to be man's final enemy; he sits at God's right hand as the firstborn of all the saved. His Resurrection is our guarantee of new life; his Ascension marks out the path to heaven that in God's loving providence we too hope to follow. He has gone to prepare a place for us and will come at the time he chooses to take us to himself (cfr. *John* 14:1-6). These truths of our faith are very familiar to us from the prayers of the funeral rite. Let us make them our

own so that we come to see our own death with the eyes of faith. If we really live our faith, when we come to die we will not regard death as the end of everything. Bodily existence will cease but only to give place to a fuller life. The passing over will be marked by hope rather than by fear.

62. We are fortunate that in Ireland so many talented and generous people take up medicine or nursing as a profession and a vocation in life. We all appreciate the spirit in which they carry out their very demanding work and we are proud of the name that Irish doctors and Irish nurses have earned the world over. It is not surprising that this spirit of generosity should find a special place in the care of the old. Grateful people all over Ireland will want us to express admiration and thanks to the sisters, nurses and the doctors who staff our hospitals, for a quality of care which goes far beyond the line of duty, and for care of the dying and help of the bereaved in the death of loved ones. All this has made sickness and bereavement for thousands a new discovery of human goodness and of Christ-like love.

Pain-Killing Drugs

63. Some people use the term euthanasia for the administration of painkilling drugs. This is unfortunate; for giving drugs to lessen pain is totally different from giving a lethal overdose of drugs to end life. Pope Pius XII dealt with the whole question of pain-killing drugs and euthanasia in 1957, in an address on "Religious and Moral Aspects of Pain Prevention in Medical Practice". What he said then is as relevant today as it was at the time. He had been asked to reply to a number of questions. One of these was: "Would it be necessary to give up (the use of drugs) if the actual effect was to shorten a span of life ?". He replied:

First, all forms of direct euthanasia, i.e., the administration of a drug in order to produce or hasten death, are unlawful, because in that case a claim is being made to dispose direct-

ly of life. If there exists no direct causal link . . . . between
the induced unconsciousness and the shortening of
life . . . .; and if, on the other hand, the actual administration of drugs brings about two distinct effects, the one the
relief of pain, the other the shortening of life, the action is
lawful.[16]

There is a clear distinction between setting out to kill a
patient and setting out to relieve a patient's pain. There is
a difference of nature and not just of motive or intention
between selecting a dose of narcotic which is calculated to
be enough to kill, and a dose which is regulated by the need
to make pain bearable.

Artificial Prolongation of Life

64. Medical personnel are nowadays called upon to take
very delicate decisions in the matter of whether to initiate
or when to discontinue artificial measures sustaining life in a
dying patient. Modern medicine makes it possible in inten-
sive care units to bring back from the edge of death patients
who not many years ago would certainly have died. Trans-
plant surgery, which is increasingly being perfected, will give
a new lease of life to many otherwise hopeless cases. To what
extent is it morally obligatory, or morally lawful, to use such
measures?

65. It is not difficult to see that it is right and even
obligatory to use such measures when, in the language of
medical ethics and of current medical science, they can be
called *ordinary* means; provided of course that they offer
reasonable hope of benefit to the patient and that their use
does not involve excessive inconvenience or suffering, or
even inordinate expense. In other words, means of pro-
longing life which can truly be called *extraordinary* are never
obligatory.

66. A very real problem arises when artificial measures of
resuscitation and life-support become death-delaying rather

than properly life-supporting. One specialist has denounced what he calls "meddlesome medicine".[17] Such medicine could be an assault on human dignity and on man's right to a dignified death. There is clearly no moral obligation to keep a body breathing and biologically alive after irreversible brain death has occurred. It is not euthanasia to decline the use of such means or even to discontinue them when it is clear that they are only death-delaying.

Community Care for the Old

67. A community cannot content itself with condemning euthanasia. It is, by that very fact, committed to a programme of care for the elderly, the handicapped, for the chronically ill and for the dying. A community calling itself Christian has a special responsibility in this regard. There has been notable progress in both thinking and planning about geriatric services in all parts of Ireland in recent years. The emphasis is placed upon domiciliary services, home helps, day hospital services; all of this with the praiseworthy end of avoiding, as far as possible, institutionalisation of the aged. This is an ideal field for collaboration between public authority and voluntary effort. The development of diocesan Social Welfare Centres and of local Community Social Service Councils provide significant evidence of a caring Christian community. State services for the elderly, as well as the handicapped, have improved enormously. Many housing programmes, both under public authority and voluntary auspices, have planned for specially designed accommodation for the elderly in proximity to necessary amenities and to normal human companionship.

68. Wherever possible, old people certainly prefer to live on in their own homes. It would be desirable that they be transferred to institutions only when home care is no longer possible. But homes for the elderly and hospitals for the

dying will always be necessary. Such homes and hospitals have benefitted from the growing social conscience of society. Public money has been more generously allocated and the grim buildings of the past are being rapidly replaced by splendidly equipped modern or modernised units. No praise could be too great for their dedicated staffs.

69. But the wider community must not devolve its responsibilities upon these units and their staffs. Apostolic and charitable groups should more and more assume responsibilities towards the sick, the elderly and the dying in support of the work of the nursing staffs. The Emperor Julian in the 4th century, calling upon pagans for a crusade to outdo Christianity, said that the strongest asset of Christians was their concern for the sick and the elderly and their respect for their dead.

Ends and Means

70. In modern society one can discern a gradual but inexorable erosion of one of the central principles of the moral law, namely the principle that the end does not justify the means. Good motives do not make wrong things right. Pursuit of personal wealth and increased gross national product tend in modern society to become ends in themselves. All means come to be thought good if they lead to these ends. Making a profit, preferably a large and quick profit, is held to justify any loss caused or any material or moral damage done to others, any untruth told, any mean advantage taken. To this extent, our wealth-and-growth-oriented society is a violent society. The ruthlessness of the land-speculator, the property-redeveloper, the business cartel; the fouling up of the physical environment by industrial pollution; the pollution of the moral environment by pornography and unchastity, the pollution of language by obscenity, all these are examples of violence done to society.

The Emperor Julian in the 4th century, calling upon
pagans for a crusade to outdo Christianity, said that
the strongest asset of Christians was their concern for
the sick and the elderly and their respect for their
dead.

So too is the abuse of power by organised groups, who, because of the particular place they occupy in industrial society, can virtually blackmail the community into conceding their terms. Thus, as has been said recently, what people earn comes to depend less on the good that they do for society than on the harm they will do to it if their claims are not met.

Political Violence

71. The theory of modern revolution is an extreme version of the philosophy that the end justifies the means. The end of the revolution (in this island, the "independence of Ireland" or "the Ulster heritage") become ends in themselves; and any and every means are held to become just in the pursuit of those ends. We have seen the most brutal crimes excused or justified on both sides by such slogans as: "This is a war and there must be innocent victims"; "This is revolution and revolution is its own morality". Political violence in the last six years has certainly constituted the most systematic and sustained attack on the sacredness of human life and on the absoluteness of the moral law to be found in the past half-century of our history.

72. We do not close our eyes to the fact that there have been two campaigns of violence, the one aimed at achieving a United Ireland by force; the other a campaign of sectarian assassination. This second campaign is still going on. It has already claimed well over 300 innocent lives. It is a matter for regret that it has not received the public attention and condemnation which it deserves.

73. As far as the other campaign is concerned, our vocabulary of moral condemnation has been virtually exhausted. Anything we could say now would seem to be merely repetitive. Nevertheless, it is our obligation to go on alerting consciences, especially those of our own flock, to evil. From

the very onset of this campaign, the Catholic Church has
pointed out unequivocally that it is utterly immoral. The
record is there to show that scarcely a month has passed
during the past five years without the campaign itself or
particular outrages for which it was responsible being condemned by us in unqualified terms.

74. In a statement issued when the campaign had scarcely
begun, we warned that these "self-appointed activists" had
absolutely no mandate from the electorate, and we condemned their campaign "in the name of God". In a statement in
1971 we enumerated the rightful claims and grievances of the
Northern minority community and condemned the various
forms of violence, discrimination and injustice of which they
had been made the victims; while also appealing to Catholics
"to realise the genuine fears and grievances of the Protestant
community". We stressed that, while painfully aware of the
minority's grievances, "*nevertheless, we condemn the violence*". We went on:

> Our main purpose in this statement, however, is to repeat
> unreservedly and without qualification, our condemnation
> of this campaign of violence. Many of those engaged in it
> may be in good faith, confused by conflicting emotions and
> ideals. But the thing itself is grievously wrong and con-
> trary to the law and spirit of Christ. Those responsible for
> it carry a grave responsibility of guilt before God.

End Justifying Means

75. But, as well as seeing the moral wrong of these campaigns, we should look more closely at the systematic moral
perversion involved in their execution. In this way we may
learn lessons from our recent history for the future moral
catechesis of our young people. Almost every kind of moral
wrong has been held justified by the end of "The Cause".
Coldly planned murders have been justified by the rhetoric

of war and revolution. Deaths and injuries of innocent
civilians have been called "unavoidable and acceptable war-
time casualties". Destruction of property worth millions of
pounds has been called "striking at economic targets".
Robbery and extorted subscriptions have been called "financing the Cause". Hijacking of vehicles, with their subsequent
destruction, became an everyday occurrence, compounded
more recently by the disgraceful practice of proxy bombing.
Most horrible of all perhaps is the no-warning bomb set off
in crowded places. Death sentences have been pronounced
and carried out without the least regard for legality or
elementary justice, and often on the merest suspicion. People
have been tortured or maimed following parodies of "trials",
in which the accused were denied all legal safeguards.

76. That all these wrongful actions have been done in the
name of patriotism or defence, law and order or freedom and
justice, does not serve in the slightest degree to make them
less wrong. In fact, the motive ensures that the wrong action
may be planned the more efficiently and carried out the more
ruthlessly. The motive may make it easier to mislead ideal-
istic young people into performing deeds of death and
destruction, which ordinarily they would totally abhor. Some
of the basest crimes of history have been done in unquestion-
ing obedience to leaders or in fanatical dedication to a
country, a revolution or a cause. Sincerity and even nobility
of intentions do not make wrong things right.

The Spiral of Violence

77. One of the tragedies of recourse to violence has been
that it unleashes a spiral of action and reaction, violence and
counter-violence, in which hate, vengeance, destruction and
death become almost a way of life. Modern revolutionary
violence enshrines the evil philosophy that intentions are the

sole determinant of the morality of action. But this evil philosophy is not confined to revolutionaries. It is espoused by organs and agencies of State as well. Reasons of security or intelligence and the need to defeat violence and restore law and order have been held to provide justification for intolerable forms of counterviolence. We have seen respectable legal authority maintain that "physical ill-treatment" — which really amounted to torture — is not brutality or cruelty unless there is "a disposition to inflict suffering coupled with indifference to or pleasure in the victim's pain".[18] Thus the end of "security", like the end of "revolution", is held to change the moral meaning of actions, in other words, to make wrong right. The end and the intention are held to justify the means. This is another example of how widespread in modern society is the tendency to judge the morality of an action, not by looking at the objective thing which is done, but at the subjective intentions or motives of the person doing it.

78. The first step towards restoring respect for the sacredness of human life and for the dignity and rights of the human person will be the conviction that some actions are evil in themselves, no matter what compassionate motive or good intentions are put forward for them, and no matter what desirable consequences are supposed to follow from them. No good intention or result will ever justify murder or robbery or torture or cruelty or racial or religious discrimination or fornication or adultery or abortion. The sacred rights of conscience, so much stressed by the Vatican Council, come from the sacred duty of conscience to obey God's law, regardless of what people say or of how many people may be shown by opinion polls to think or act differently, and no matter what the consequences; and to refuse to do evil, regardless of how fashionable it has become, or of who approves or who commands it, and no matter what gain it brings.

Death or Life ?

79. Modern society believes that it is choosing a better quality of life. But in fact, it sometimes shows a strange inclination towards a death-wish. A contraceptive mentality is easily followed by the abortive mentality; and both of these are concerned with rejecting life. We have said that the arguments given for abortion are parallel to those used in favour of euthanasia. A recent writer, advocating euthanasia, has spoken of "planned death", and has hailed "the comfort of a death-conditioned society".[19] Such language is a strange comment on the compassionate society and its dedication to the quality of life. From birth control to death control, from planned birth to planned death, there seems to be a logical progress; but it is a logic of death, not life. This cannot be the way of the Christian. One of the earliest Christian writings, after the New Testament itself, namely the *Didache*, calls the way of the Christian "the way of life", and opposes it to the pagan "way of death". The writer applies his title specifically to the Christian refusal of abortion and infanticide. The Book of Wisdom says:

> Death was not God's doing,
> He takes no pleasure in the extinction of the living.
> To be — for this he created all . . . .
> But the godless call with deed and word for Death,
> Counting him friend, they wear themselves out for him,
> With him they make a pact,
> And are fit to be his partners (*Wisdom* 1:13, 16).

Moses said to the people:

> I set before you life or death, blessing or curse. Choose life, then, so that you and your descendants may live, in the love of the Lord your God (*Deuteronomy* 30:19).

That is still the choice and the commitment and the privilege of a people who believe in the Living God.

Part Three:
LOVE IS FOR LIFE

Thou Shalt Love

80. We cannot separate Christian concern for the sacredness of life and specifically for the sacredness of unborn life from the Christian understanding of sexuality. Both are part of the one mystery of love and life. Christian sexual morality does not consist only of forbidding things or avoiding things. After all, one could avoid a whole list of wrong actions outside or inside of marriage, and yet be very immoral and un-Christian in one's relationships. Christianity is a positive thing. It means saying "Yes" to God in Christ; and saying "Yes" to the love which he blesses and to the life which he gives. It is when one understands life, love, sex and marriage in their full Christian and human meaning that one sees that certain forms of behaviour are a betrayal of love and an offence against life; and that is why they are wrong. The adulterer, for example, betrays both the love he owes his wife and the love he owes to his own children. In Christian morality, the prohibition, "Thou shalt not", is always a consequence of the positive command, "Thou shalt love".

Wholesome View of Human Sexuality

81. One must always keep in view the total Christian vision of love and sexuality. Whenever sexual morality has come to be isolated from this context, it has been damaged by the process. A wholesome view of sex is one which tries to see it in the whole of its human and spiritual reality, and tries to see it in the wholeness of the Christian calling.

82. In the past perhaps some people tended to discuss the

morality of sex as if what chiefly mattered was the physical structure of the sexual activity, and as though the emotional, human and personal aspect of sexuality were less important. Marriage was sometimes discussed by moralists mainly in terms of 'marriage rights'. This would be a very limited view of the matter; for, between husband and wife, sexual intercourse is not only a right or a duty but is also an act which seals and expresses a mutual and generous love. The sexual aspect of marriage has sometimes been feared by some or endured by others as a condition of marriage. On the other hand it has been selfishly indulged in by others as an unconditional right of marriage, without consideration for the feelings or sensitivity of the marriage partner. Too few see it as something good and holy in marriage, blessed by the sacrament and sanctifying the partners.

83. While recognising errors in past attitudes to sex, we must also recognise that we may nowadays be making different but equally unfortunate mistakes. Christian morality, as some presented it, may have seemed at times to be too much preoccupied with sex. There has recently been a reaction against this exaggeration, and this is a healthy reaction. But we must be careful not to fall now into the opposite error of regarding sexual morality as unimportant. The authentic Christian teaching on the morality of sex has not fundamentally changed and will not change. Sexuality is an area of profound importance, not only in itself and in its bearing on the happiness of persons, but in its significance for the entire development of the moral personality.

Male and Female He Created Them

84. Men and women were created male and female by God. Here is how the Book of Genesis puts it:

> God created man in the image of himself, in the image of God he created him, male and female he created them (*Genesis* 1:27).

It is indicated here that man bears the image of God, not alone in his spiritual soul, but also in his body. This also is created by God, and reflects God's love and goodness and holiness. God looked on sexuality too, with everything else that he had made, and saw that "indeed it was very good" (*Genesis* 1:31). The original goodness of our bodies as created by the hand of God is restored and elevated by baptism, which gives them a share in the holiness and beauty of the risen body of Christ.

85. Sexuality is one of the most powerful of our biological and emotional endowments. It is one of the deepest constituents of personality. Men and women are complementary to one another, not just in their physical sexuality, but also in their psychology, their sensibility, and even, in important respects, in their spirituality. The words of Genesis have a profound meaning:

> The Lord God said, "It is not good that the man should be alone. I will make him a help-mate like to himself" (*Genesis* 2:13).

86. It is above all in marriage that the companionship and mutual help of man and woman find their highest expression. Sexual union should be the physical expression of the deepest emotional and personal relationship between man and woman. Sexual union is a source of new life and of the profound human experience of parenthood and of parent-child relationship. Sexuality is, indeed, an area in which man experiences new heights in his existence and realises in wonder his longing for the infinite. Even at the level of human experience, sexual love can be an intimation of the nature of God who is Love. The language of sexual love has indeed been used by God himself in the Bible as an analogy for his relations with the people whom he loves. Sexual love puts men in touch with the mystery of life and of creation; and the experience of parenthood and of filial love can be intimations of our relationship with God our Father.

87. All of this provides sufficient explanation of why the Christian must be concerned about sexual attitudes and behaviour. The views about sexuality in modern society have changed radically. In the last century, attitudes were often puritanical, and at times even hypocritical. Nowadays people are more open and indeed frequently more honest. But there is also much in the contemporary attitude to sex which must be rejected. Modern culture often dehumanises and trivialises sex, robbing it of its mystery and sacredness, and indeed denying its deepest human meaning and beauty. In the consumer society, sex tends to become a marketable product. It becomes treated as a thing, isolated from the person as a whole and from respect for persons. Pictures of the female body are used to sell any and every kind of product. It is good that women have recently been protesting more vigorously about the way in which they are projected as sex objects, rather than treated as persons in their own right. When sexuality is thus cheapened, men and women themselves become diminished and dehumanised. Not only is sexuality itself debased in the process, but men and women are in danger of losing the great power for healing and enrichment and uplifting which a properly human and Christian attitude to sexuality can bring. The much-vaunted sexual liberation of our time often turns into new forms of enslavement of the person.

Modern Forms of Idolatry

88. St. Paul frequently warns us not to throw away the true freedom which Christ has brought us and revert to old forms of enslavement to passion and to false gods. In one passage, he says: "Put to death what is earthly in you: immorality, impurity, passion, evil desire, and covetousness, which is idolatry" (*Colossians* 3:5). The use of the word "idolatry" recalls Christ's phrase, "You cannot serve God and Mammon". Often in the Bible, man's surrender to his own

It is above all in marriage that the companionship
and mutual help of man and woman find their highest
expression. The experience of parenthood and of
filial love can be intimations of our relationship
with God our Father.

passions is compared with idolatry or the worshipping of false gods. In particular, idolatry is seen as a form of prostitution or fornication; and in turn, impurity is seen as a form of idolatry. Modern man would be shocked to be accused of idolatry. But we have to ask whether the worship of false gods really has been abolished in our Western way of life. Perhaps money, alcohol, drugs and sex are being given a place and a status in modern secular society which is not too different from the place occupied by the gods of money, wine and sex in pagan times.

Celibacy and Consecrated Virginity

89. It is suggested sometimes that the Church downgraded marriage and took a low view of sex because of her esteem for virginity and her desire for celibate vocations. This is not so. The Church's esteem for virginity comes from Christ himself. He was born of a virgin mother. He himself chose to remain unmarried. He said that the life of the Resurrection was a virginal life and that virginity was an anticipation already here on earth of the future Resurrection. If the Church has always recognised the superiority of virginity, as being in itself, and for those called by God to it, a higher form of life than marriage, this is simply part of her fidelity to Christ himself.[20]

90. But Christ also defied the taboos of the culture of his time in showing his respect for women. He spoke openly and alone with them, as no rabbi would do. He visited women as special friends. He scandalised pious people by associating with women who were known to be sinners. He honoured marriage with his presence and his first miracle; indeed he used the occasion of a marriage to advance the hour of the manifestation of his glory and the outpouring of his grace. He made marriage a sacrament.

91. Virginity and marriage are not in contrast or conflict

with one another. The more marriage is honoured as a source of grace and a means to holiness, the more virginity will be esteemed and the more will virginal vocations be desired. In turn, the more virginity is honoured, the greater will be the respect for marriage and the more will people be motivated to work for its more authentic living. Many priests and religious are among those actively working in Ireland today to make marriage more esteemed and honoured, and to improve services for families.

92. Reverence for sexuality, for marriage and for virginity all come alike from Our Lord himself; and in all this St. Paul is his faithful disciple. The greatest movement of genuine liberation for women that history has ever known was that introduced into the world by Our Lord. The figure of Mary, Virgin and Mother, had a decisive role in history. It did much to civilise men's attitudes towards women and to promote respect for women as persons in their own right and as partners and associates rather than possessions of their menfolk.

Marriage and Responsible Love

93. The Christian's answer to modern misunderstanding of the true nature of sexuality and of love will be found in the Vatican Council's Constitution *On the Church in the Modern World*. Pope Paul's Encyclical, *Humanae Vitae,* also bears witness to the true and full significance of human sexuality, within the Christian understanding of the mystery of love and of life. *Humanae Vitae* is often discussed without in fact being read. There is very much more in this encyclical than is popularly supposed. Summaries of it are often selective; discussion of it is often one-sided. Those who read the whole text will find in it an inspiring description of human life in the eyes of God and of human sexuality as the source of this life. The Encyclical gives us a new appreciation of the love relationship which is marriage. It is marked by a high esteem for sexuality as expressing and fostering this married love.

The Encyclical teaches that sexual union, to be fully true to itself, requires that generosity of spirit by which one surrenders oneself in loving one's partner and in welcoming new life.

94.   The Church has always taught, and the Vatican Council and Pope Paul repeat, that sexual intercourse is completely truthful only when it expresses the unconditionally faithful love of husband and wife and their generous readiness to welcome new life.   These two terms, "love" and "life" are the anchor points of sexual morality. Partnership and parenthood are the two terms which give the key to the meaning of human sexuality. These are so linked with one another that sexual intercourse can be seen to be fully human and to have true fulfilment only within marriage. Sexual intercourse is the symbol of total mutual surrender and union between a man and a woman. The symbol states an untruth unless that man and woman are in fact committed to one another and united with one another within the security and the fidelity of a life-long partnership. This surrender and this union imply openness to the new life which would express the shared love and the united lives of man and wife. It is only within marriage that new life can be fully wanted and welcomed and offered the best conditions for growth to maturity. The first condition for a future society of loved children and loving persons is a renewed respect for the holiness of marriage. Whatever weakens marriage weakens society and endangers the future of civilisation.

95. Words describing the conditions for authentic married love seem cold and stilted. In real life, the things they describe become a single, warm and living whole. In real life, husband and wife, parents and children, are united in a single circle of love. Man and woman become more than ever husband and wife when they become father and mother; man and woman become more than ever parents the more they are lovingly united with one another as husband and

wife. In the daily experience of family life, partnership and parenthood are not distinct or separate and cannot be opposed to each other.

96. The Second Vatican Council spoke of marriage as "a community of love". The first duty of husband and wife is to develop and perfect their love for each other. This requires mutual consideration and concern, it requires self-control, which means control of one's selfish impulses. It requires self-denial, which means the constant effort to overcome one's self-centredness. Continuous effort is needed by both husband and wife to acquire that sensitivity to the feelings and the needs of the other, in all spheres and in all moods, which is the proof of genuine love. Selfishness speaks and thinks and acts in terms of "I". Successful marriage leads partners to think and speak and act in terms of "We". Successful marriage, therefore, requires a continued struggle to overcome selfishness.

97. In earlier days, sexual harmony in marriage did not receive much attention. In our days, the danger instead is that people will speak and act as though physical sexual harmony is the only thing that matters. Some approach marriage as though sexual success would make up for all other failings, and atone for all faults. This is untrue. Married people's sexual happiness will be the result of their loving care and concern for one another's general happiness. Sexual intercourse will express love only if one's whole way of life expresses love. If couples cease to talk to one another, to listen to one another, to go out together, to share the same interests together, they will become strangers sharing the same house; and sexual intercourse will actually deepen rather than remove the hurt of their estranged silence. It is perhaps men who need most to be reminded of this. Their tenderness and thoughtfulness sometimes end with the honeymoon. Irish married men can remain bachelors at

heart, happiest in male company outside the home and not trying to build even a friendship, much less a loving marriage, with their wives.

98. A particular shadow falls over marriage in this country because of the drinking habits of our people. Excessive drinking is without question one of the greatest sources of marital unhappiness and breakdown in Ireland. Over indulgence often begins from an irresponsible attitude towards married love and family life; it rapidly aggravates this irresponsibility. The first requirement of love is to try to become a better person for the sake of the other whom one loves, so that one may be able to enrich the life of the other and become in turn more worthy of the other's love. Love has been called "the joy of sacrificing oneself for the happiness of another".

99. What counts more than anything is the kind of person and the kind of Christian one is in one's whole attitude to life. Marriages come under strain quite often because of some defects in the general moral character of the partners, rather than because of some specific marriage problem. What emerges as a sexual or emotional difficulty may well be a symptom of a much more general defect in personality or failure in relationships — for example, some deep-seated immaturity, aggressiveness, selfishness, insensitivity to others, pleasure-seeking or self-indulgence. Psychologists will use their own technical terms to describe these defects; but there can be also moral guilt involved.

100. There are few moral failings affecting married life which are not covered by the traditional list of the Seven Deadly Sins — pride, avarice, lust, anger, gluttony, envy, sloth. St. Paul's description of the results of self-indulgence also provides an important list of things to be avoided in marriage. His enumeration includes "sexual irresponsibil-

The first condition for a future society of loved children and loving persons is a renewed respect for the holiness of marriage.

ity . . . . wrangling, jealousy, bad temper and quarrels, disagreements, envy, drunkenness and similar things". Opposed to these stands his list of "the fruits of the Spirit"; and married people could well take this list as a charter for their married life. This is what St. Paul says: "What the Spirit brings is very different: love, joy, peace, patience, kindness, goodness, trustfulness, gentleness and self-control" (*Galatians* 5:19-23).

101. Writing to the Ephesians, St. Paul speaks directly to husbands. Here is what he tells them: "Husbands should love their wives just as Christ loved the Church and sacrificed himself for her to make her holy (*Ephesians* 5:25). This exhortation applies, of course, to wives as well. It is a reminder to each that their love for one another must be a self-sacrificing love, like Christ's love for them. If husband and wife wish to learn how they are to love one another, they will learn it on their knees together before a crucifix. This is how Christ loves them. This is how they are to love one another. We could use the words of a great French preacher, Lacordaire, and say that husband and wife must each try to become for the other "the other's particular Christ".

102. This is no vague pious exhortation. It is the direct application to married life of Christ's command that we should love one another as he has loved us. St. Paul teaches how concrete and realistic this commandment is. In the unforgettable thirteenth chapter of his First Letter to the Corinthians, he says: "Love is always patient and kind; it is never jealous; love is never boastful or conceited, it is never rude or selfish, it does not take offence, and is not resentful. Love takes no pleasure in other people's sins but delights in the truth; it is always ready to excuse, to trust, to hope, and to endure whatever comes. Love does not come to an end" (1 *Corinthians* 13: 4-8). All Christian married people, as well as couples preparing for marriage, should read these

words carefully and often. They should each examine their
treatment of the other by these words. It would be better
still that each couple should, from time to time, as a couple.
read these words together and pray about them together.

Education in Human Relationships

103. There is certainly need for much preparation and
education for marriage. This will obviously include what is
called "sex education". But certain kinds of sex education
would only aggravate the problems rather than solve them.
Mere instruction in the physiology of sex, isolated from its
emotional and personal values, and especially from its
spiritual and moral aspects, would not in fact be education
for marriage at all; for marriage is a union of two lives and
two whole persons, not just of two bodies. Indeed this would
not even be instruction about human sexuality. Human
sexuality is marked by the immortal spirit of man and not
just by bodily instinct. Shakespeare alluded to this when he
spoke of lust as "the expense of spirit in a waste of shame".

104. Sex education must always be placed in a spiritual and
religious setting. For us Christians, it must always be in the
context of Christian teaching. Scripture and the faith in fact
provide the most perfect setting for this education.   The
story of the Annunciation shows how virginal innocence in
Mary does not exclude reverent knowledge of the facts of
sexuality and of birth. The knowledge that our bodies are
the temple of the Holy Spirit shows that purity is simply
respect for the holiness of the place where God dwells. The
sublime doctrine of baptism teaches that our bodies are
consecrated and sealed for Christ. Indeed they are made
parts of the sacred Body of Christ. St. Paul concludes that
fornication is taking the body of Christ which we are and
bringing it into contact with sin and shame. Christian teaching, therefore, combines simple and joyful and thankful

acceptance of sexuality as God's gift, with complete rejection of the abuse of this gift. Parents and all those responsible for the formation of young people, especially in today's world, are gravely failing our youth if they do not ensure that the proper Christian attitudes towards sexuality are imparted to them at all appropriate stages.

105. We repeat that sexuality can never be isolated from the wider aspects of personal relationships. What is above all needed is preparation of young people for mature personal relationships. There is some reason to think that this aspect of education may be more neglected in boys' schools at present than in girls' schools. However this may be, it is vital for both boys and girls. No amount of academic success will replace this ability to form mature personal relationships and especially to make mature marriages.

106. As Christians, of course, we will remember that all our relationships with others, and above all relationships between married partners, must be, as St. Paul never tires of repeating, "in Christ Jesus". The basis of all personal relations and of all marriages should be our own personal relationship with Jesus Christ. That we should come to know him as a living person, our most loved and trusted friend, our daily companion, our model for living — this is the basis and the aim of all Christian education. It is the condition of all Christian maturity. It is from Christ that we learn how to relate maturely to others. It is he who teaches us how to love in a way that is "fully mature, with the fullness of Christ himself" (*Ephesians* 4:13).

Part Four:
LOVE GIVES LIFE

Welcomed and Loved

107. Love in marriage ordinarily finds its highest fulfilment in bringing new life into the world. When God blesses marriage with children, these should be, and should grow up knowing themselves to be, the living expression of the love of husband and wife for one another. The child usually bears traces of the physical appearance and the character traits of both the husband and the wife, blended together in a new human face and personality. The child is thus a new bond of love between the partners. The love of husband and wife lives on in a third mutually loved and shared little one. In the child and around the child, husband and wife become in a new way one. In a truly Christian society and family, every child should be, and should feel itself to be, a loved and welcomed child.

108. The term 'wanted child' is much used nowadays. "Every child a wanted child" is indeed a noble ideal. But the term can be ambiguous. "Wanting" a child is not the matter of one's emotion of a day, but of one's attitude to life. At the emotional level, the attitude to a pregnancy can fluctuate with changing health or changing moods, before, during and after the pregnancy. It is not by such changing moods that one's deeper attitudes are measured. It is not on shifting sands like these that a child's security and maturity can be built. "Wanting" a child is not so much something one feels as something one does, or even something one is. It would be better to speak of accepting a child from God as a gift of his love, than of "wanting" it. It would be more natural to speak of welcomed and loved children than of

"wanted" children. The loving and the welcoming must go on all through life. They depend on the kind of person and parent one chooses to be, and not on any set of techniques.

109. The truly "wanted" child is one who is assured of acceptance into a family of loved and loving members, with all the security and stability which this implies. The first claim that a child has upon its parents is that, from its conception, it should be welcomed and loved by them. The normal condition for growth to mature adulthood for a child is parents who love it. But the child just as urgently needs parents who love one another. Parents owe it to their children not only that they love their children, but that they love one another around their children. Only homes that are filled with an atmosphere of love can guarantee the development of mature personalities. Only loving homes will produce young people who will be capable, in their turn, of entering into mature relationships with others. Marriages, families and homes of this kind are the most precious asset of human society. One of the first duties of society is to protect, support and assist marriage and the family.

110. Couples who wish to have children but are unable to have them can also have complete fulfilment in their marriage. God's blessing is realised for them in other ways. Their involuntary childlessness may give them more opportunities for charitable or apostolic work or for other forms of service to others. Many such couples adopt a child, thereby giving a loving home and a future to children who might otherwise be deprived of both.

The Contraceptive Mentality

111. This ideal of marriage and the family is placed under severe strain in modern society. It can scarcely survive except it is sustained by Christian faith and by the Christian vision of the mystery and meaning of sexuality. This

Christian vision includes the full reality and richness of sexuality as God created it, while raising this to a new level. It is to this vision that Pope Paul appeals in his Encyclical, *Humanae Vitae*. It is because of this Christian and integrally human vision that he takes issue with contraceptive methods and programmes of birth regulation.

112. "Contraceptive mentality" is a suitable term for a whole pattern of wrong attitudes and priorities in respect of marriage and parenthood. The term stands for the invasion of Christian attitudes to life and to marriage by typical materialist values. The contraceptive mentality is characterised by lack of generosity of spirit and of readiness to assume responsibility. It tends to regard comfort, wealth, worldly success and pleasure as the aims of life. The contraceptive mentality contradicts the Christian understanding of family life. It is fundamentally opposed to the Christian concept of responsible parenthood. In contemporary experience, this contraceptive mentality is directly associated with the use of artificial methods of contraception. It can even, in the end, bring with it a prejudice against new life. It is significant that many of those who have been most prominent in campaigns for contraception are also found among the leading advocates of abortion. For some of these, abortion is openly recognised as "the second line of defence against unwanted pregnancy". Furthermore, there is evidence that some pills or appliances (intra-uterine devices or "I.U.D.'s", for example) commonly supplied as contraceptives are in fact primarily abortifacients. Advocates of contraception tend to ignore or conceal this evidence.

Acceptable Methods of Birth Regulation

113. There are morally acceptable methods of birth spacing and birth regulation, which, on the contrary, belong to a Christian philosophy of life and a Christian understanding of

responsible parenthood. Pope Paul commended these methods of regulation of birth as a "discipline proper to the purity of married couples". He went on:

> It demands continual effort, yet, thanks to its beneficent influence, husband and wife fully develop their personalities, being enriched with spiritual values. Such a discipline bestows upon family life the fruits of serenity and peace . . . .; it favours attention for one's partner, helps both parties to drive out selfishness, the enemy of true love; and deepens their sense of responsibility (*Humanae Vitae* 21).

Abstinence too can at times be a genuine and necessary expression of married love. Many who are practising the above methods, even when they are experiencing difficulties, will confirm, from their own experience, the words of Pope Paul. On the other hand, the use of immoral methods has been known to lead gradually, as Pope Paul predicted, to a loss of respect by the husband for the wife and to a feeling on her part that she has become the object of her husband's satisfaction rather than his "respected and beloved companion" (*Humanae Vitae*, 17).

114. Research into these natural methods is continuing all the time, so that their reliability is gradually increasing. Continuous propaganda against them tends to create a quite unjustifiable lack of confidence. Natural methods of birth regulation differ essentially from artificial methods. The former are based upon growing knowledge of God's own design for the cycle of reproduction. By their use, men and women can enter more fully into the loving designs of God, and can, even more consciously, become "pro-creators" with God in his plan that men "fill the earth and conquer it" (*Genesis* 1:28). In thus co-operating in God's plan for the earth, Christians will also remember that they are sharing in God's eternal plan to "bring everything together under Christ as head", for the eternal praising of God's glory in heaven by those to whom he gave life on earth through generously loving parents (cfr. *Ephesians* 1:10-14).

The Christian and Birth Regulation

115. The Second Vatican Council had this to say about generous parenthood:

> Trusting in divine providence and refining the spirit of sacrifice, married Christians glorify the Creator and strive toward fulfilment in Christ when, with a generous human and Christian sense of responsibility, they acquit themselves of the duty to procreate. Among the couples who fulfil their God-given task in this way, those merit special mention who with wise and common deliberation, and with a gallant heart, undertake to bring up suitably even a relatively large family (Constitution, *Gaudium et Spes, On the Church in the Modern World*, 50).

It is necessary to recall this today, when the term 'responsible parenthood' is being annexed in modern society for the small family 'planned' by the use of contraceptives; and when strong social pressures are mounted to induce couples to conform to this new norm, even to the point of making them feel 'irresponsible' if they do not conform.

116. It is not, however, the number of children which is the primary consideration. Responsible parenthood is more a matter of the attitude of generosity, readiness for sacrifice, prayerfulness and trust in Providence which underlies decisions about the size and pattern of family. The same Constitution of the Second Vatican Council, on the Church in the Modern World, from which we have just quoted, says:

> Parents will fulfil their task with human and Christian responsibility . . . . thoughtfully taking into account both their welfare and that of their children, those already born and those that may be foreseen. They will consider both the material and the spiritual conditions of the times, as well as of their own state in life. They will consider the interests of the family group, of temporal society, and of the Church itself (50).

These positive attitudes and motives may operate also in marriages where the couples desire children but cannot have them. Parents can also preserve this welcoming attitude

5. Human Life Is Sacred

towards children even when, at least at this time, medical or other considerations indicate that a child should not be conceived.

117. Where the method of birth regulation is concerned, the Second Vatican Council said:

> The moral aspect of any procedure does not depend solely on sincere intention or on the evaluation of motives. It must be determined by objective standards. These, based on the nature of the human person and his acts, preserve the full sense of mutual self-giving and human procreation in the context of true love. Such a goal cannot be achieved unless the virtue of conjugal chastity is sincerely practised. Relying on these principles, members of the Church may not undertake methods of regulating procreation which are found blameworthy by the teaching authority of the Church in its unfolding of the divine law (*The Church in the Modern World*, 51).

118. Pope Paul, in *Humanae Vitae*, restated the Church's traditional teaching about birth regulation. He reaffirmed, in absolute terms, the immorality both of sterilisation and of contraception. Having stated the Church's position on the evil of abortion, he says:

> Equally to be condemned, as the Magisterium of the Church has affirmed on various occasions, is direct sterilisation, whether of the man or of the woman, whether permanent or temporary. Similarly excluded is any action, which either before, at the moment of, or after sexual intercourse, is specifically intended to prevent procreation, whether as an end or as a means (14).

Regretfully we must note that sterilising operations are being carried out in some places in this country. Sterilisation as a contraceptive measure is condemned by the Pope in unqualified terms and is unacceptable to the instructed Catholic conscience.

119. These absolute and uncompromising statements of Pope Paul are an unambiguous witness to moral truth and value, particularly in an area where passion and selfishness

or prejudice may blind people's perception of that Christian value. These words of the Pope reflect the Church's awareness, accumulated and deepened over centuries of inherited experience, of man's tendency to distort the meaning of his sexuality by manipulating the sources of life for his own pleasure and convenience. The Encyclical is a prophetic call to all men of good will to recognise that in man, by the Creator's decree, sex is intrinsically linked with love and life, a link which man breaks at his peril.

120. Surely, if one looks around the modern world, one sees that for very many today a tragic abuse and waste are being made of love between the sexes. The mechanical repetition of the word love in film and pop-song, the portrayal of love in purely bodily, hedonistic and sexual terms in magazine and newspaper, underline how shallow these deep human experiences have become for many people. *Humanae Vitae* proclaims that human sexuality has a deeper meaning, that it belongs essentially to the mystery of married love and of new life. Pope Paul's Encyclical is a reminder that when man dehumanises sex by taking it out of this context of marriage and new life, he dehumanises himself.

121. Pope Paul stressed in this connection the need to create an atmosphere favourable to chastity. Chastity is a term which is not in favour in the modern world. It is simply the name for the virtue, that is the grace and the strength, which protect human sexuality from everything that would soil it or degrade it. It is "a gift from God with a power that enables the will . . . . to integrate the sex drive into the entirety of the Christian personality".[21] Pope Paul calls attention to the duty, particularly of educators and of all those responsible for the common good, to promote "education in chastity". He declares that the exploitation of sex in the modern media, as well as every form of pornography, "must arouse the frank and unanimous reaction of all those who are solicitous for the progress of civilisation

and the defence of the supreme good of the human spirit"
(*Humanae Vitae*, 21). Part at least of the storm which followed
Humanae Vitae, and which still attends any recall of it, is due
to the atmosphere unfavourable to chastity which has been
created in recent times, particularly in the Western world.
Part of the difficulty in living its message is undoubtedly due
to the pressures which the prevailing secular atmosphere
exerts upon Christians.

122. The noble and beautiful ideal of Christian marriage
cannot be realised except in a life of faith, prayer and sacrifice.
Pope Paul remarks:

> We do not at all intend to hide the sometimes serious
> difficulties inherent in the life of Christian married persons;
> for them, as for everyone else, "the gate is narrow and the
> way is hard that leads to life". But the hope of that life
> must illuminate their way, as with courage they strive to
> live with wisdom, justice and piety, in this present time,
> knowing that the figure of this world passes away . . . .
> Let them implore divine assistance by persevering prayer;
> above all, let them draw from the source of grace and
> charity in the Eucharist (*Humanae Vitae* 25).

Prophetic and Pastoral

123. The judgment on contraception in *Humanae Vitae* was
interpreted by some as harsh and as out of touch with the
difficult human situation in which many married couples have
to live. But in proclaiming God's design for human sexuality,
the Church does not lack understanding of and tolerance for
human weakness. She combines prophetic witness to moral
principles with the pastoral witness of compassion. In this,
the Church is following the example of Christ himself. As
Pope Paul puts it:

> If on the one hand it is an outstanding manifestation of
> charity towards souls to omit nothing from the saving
> doctrine of Christ, still on the other hand this must always
> be joined with tolerance and charity. Of this the Lord

himself in his conversation and dealings with men has left an example. For when he came, not to judge but to save the world, was he not bitterly severe towards sin, but patient and abounding in mercy towards sinners? (*Humanae Vitae* 29).

124. When the confessor or pastor is asked, "Is contraception wrong?", he must state clearly, "It is wrong". In assessing the degree of moral failure in a particular case, of course, one must not exclude from this area (the area of contraception) the traditional moral principles which recognise that circumstances may sometimes diminish or even exclude subjective guilt (or culpability). It is a grave responsibility of conscience on the penitent and on the confessor to decide whether, or to what extent, culpability has been diminished in a particular case. In all circumstances, the faithful should continue to have recourse to God's mercy and to his strengthening grace in the Sacrament of Penance.

125. Many moral problems — whether it be in the area of justice, of charity, of business, of politics, of sex or whatever — can be perplexing and in human terms may offer no easy solution. One must remember that it is precisely in coping with problems and indeed in suffering through them that one develops as a person and as a Christian. It is in this way that, in St. Paul's words, "We live by the truth and in love", and "grow in all ways into Christ", becoming "fully mature with the fulness of Christ himself" (*Ephesians* 4:16, 13). A moral problem should be seen not just as an obstacle to the moral life but as an opportunity for growth in that life. The life of the Church herself is one of ongoing and never-ending renewal. The life of the individual Christian is one of ceaselessly renewed effort, of endless beginning again. Success for the Christian lies in refusing to give up the effort, refusing to admit defeat. It is victory through and beyond failure. In the struggle, we are sustained by the all-powerful Spirit which raised Jesus from the dead. We are given the certitude of victory by "Christ among us, our hope of glory" (*Colossians*

1:25). Every Christian can say with St. Paul: "It is for this that I struggle wearily on, helped only by his power driving me irresistibly" (*Colossians* 1:27, 29). The Christian life is much more a matter of constantly knowing one's need for God's forgiveness than of supposing one does not need forgiveness. The real failure is that of the Pharisee, thanking God that "one is not like the rest of mankind".

126. In preaching the moral life of the Christian, the Church is giving witness to a Kingdom which is not of this world. She cannot conform to the world's standards, where these are inspired by an opposite conception of the meaning of human life. She will have to stand apart, and often alone, in order to be a light to the world. This is the witness which Christians as individuals and as couples and as families are called to give in the field of sexual morality and respect for new life. This witness was never more necessary than today. In giving it, Christians will frequently find themselves out of step with the laws of secular society and with the conventions by which much of the world chooses to live. St. John's advice to the Christians of his time needs to be recalled today: "It is not every spirit, my dear people, that you can trust; test them, to see if they come from God; there are many false prophets, now, in the world" (1 *John* 4:1). As St. Paul puts it: "Finally, brothers, fill your minds with everything that is true, everything that is noble, everything that is good and pure, everything that we love and honour and everything that can be thought virtuous or worthy of praise . . .; then the God of peace will be with you" (*Philippians* 4:8-9).

127. Few things are more necessary for all of us in the Church in these days than a renewal of Christian joy and hope. St. Paul's prayer for the Church was: "May the God of hope bring you such joy and peace in your faith that the power of the Holy Spirit will remove all bounds to hope"

(*Romans* 15:13).   In its Dogmatic Constitution on the Church
the Second Vatican Council said:

> The Church, "like a pilgrim in a foreign land, presses
> forward amid the persecutions of the world and the consol-
> ations of God" (St. Augustine), announcing the cross and
> death of the Lord until he comes (cf. 1 *Corinthians* 11: 26).
> By the power of the Risen Lord, she is given strength to
> overcome patiently and lovingly the afflictions and hard-
> ships which assail her from within and without, and to
> show forth in the world the mystery of the Lord in a
> faithful though shadowed way, until at the last it will be
> revealed in total splendour (no. 8).

Re-echoing this message, we express our concluding message
to you in the words of St. Paul: "There is no need to worry;
but if there is anything you need, pray for it, asking God for
it with prayer and thanksgiving; and that peace of God,
which is so much greater than we can understand, will guard
your hearts and your thoughts, in Christ Jesus" (*Philippians*
4: 6-7).

On behalf of the Hierarchy of Ireland,
✝WILLIAM CARDINAL CONWAY
Archbishop of Armagh
✝DERMOT RYAN
Archbishop of Dublin
✝JOSEPH CUNNANE
Archbishop of Tuam
✝THOMAS MORRIS
Archbishop of Cashel

Feast of St. Joseph the Worker May 1st 1975

[1] A useful study of the Hippocratic Oath is that of Professor Louis Portes of the French Academy of Medicine. It appeared in *Cahiers Laennec*, Lethielleux, Paris, 1951. A translation of the complete text of the Oath is on pp. 3-4.

[2] For the complete text, see Portes, *op. cit.*, p. 33.

[3] Professor Ian Donald, Regius Professor of Midwifery, University of Glasgow. The quotation is from his contribution to a pamphlet of the Order of Christian Unity, 1973.

See article, "Professional Staff Reaction to Abortion Work", by Marianne Such-Baer, a psychiatric social worker, in *Social Casework*, the journal of the Family Service Association of America, New York, vol. 55, no. 7, July 1974, pp. 435-441. The writer favours abortion; but it is significant that she sees this need for counselling and attitude-training for abortion workers to enable them to overcome instinctive repugnance.

[5] See *Abortion Law Reformed*, by Madeleine Simms and Keith Hindell, Peter Owen, London, 1971. The phrases quoted will be found on pp. 25, 122, 127, 130.

[6] Preamble to the Declaration of the Rights of the Child, published by the United Nations Office of Public Information (OPI/422-03306), February 1973.

[7] *Apologeticum* IX 8.

[8] See Michael Scott, *Abortion: the Facts*, Darton, Longman and Todd, London, 1973, p. 21.

[9] Some of the literature is reviewed by Dr. Noel Walsh in his article, "In Defence of the Unborn", in *Studies*, Winter 1972, pp. 303-314. See also Dr. Margaret and Arthur Wynn, "Some consequences of induced abortion to children born subsequently" (Foundation for Education and Research into Child-bearing, 1973).

[10] Madeleine Simms and Keith Hindell, *Abortion Law Reformed*, p. 22.

[11] no. 51.

[12] J. A. Gresham, "A time to be born and a time to die", in *Euthanasia and the Right to Die*, edited by A. B. Downing, Peter Owen, London, 1969, p. 148.

[13] *The Last Achievement*, by Dr. Willem Berger, Grail Publications, 1975.

[14] Dr. Robert Twycross, "A Plea for Eu Thanatos", in *The Month*, February 1975, p. 36. This article is interesting in that, although a thorough-going repudiation of euthanasia, it was written for, and won, a competition organised in 1972 by the Voluntary Euthanasia Society.

[15] Dr. Robert Twycross, *loc. cit.*, p. 41.

[16] Text reprinted by the Catholic Truth Society of Ireland, 1957, p. 23.

[17] Dr. Robert Twycross, *loc. cit.*, pp. 39-40.

[18] *Report of the enquiry into allegations against the security forces of physical brutality in Northern Ireland arising out of events on the 9th August*, 1971, Chairman Sir Edmund Compton, GCB KBE, Her Majesty's Stationery Office, London, 1971, Cmnd. 4823, no. 105.

[19] Mary Rose Barrington, "A Plea for Suicide", in *Euthanasia and the Right to Die*, p. 169.

[20] See Second Vatican Council, Decree on Priestly Formation, *Optatam Totius*, 10: "Seminarians should be duly aware of the duties and dignity of Christian Marriage . . . Let them perceive as well the superiority of virginity consecrated to Christ". Cfr. Decree on the Ministry and Life of Priests, *Presbyterorum Ordinis*, 16.

[21] *A Guide to Formation in Priestly Celibacy*, issued by the Sacred Congregation for Christian Education, Rome, 1974, no. 22.

SUPPLEMENTARY NOTES

1. TO PARAGRAPH 19

The question of the time of "animation" or "ensoulment" of the fetus, or of the "infusion" of the human soul, does not essentially affect the moral issue. This question was long debated by medieval theologians. It has begun to be discussed again in modern moral theology. But the wrongness of abortion is quite independent of the outcome of this discussion. To act in such a way as to prevent the ensoulment of a fetus – an ensoulment which will occur in the natural process of fetal development unless someone forcibly interrupts this development – this would be just as much an attack on human life as to kill an already ensouled fetus. To bring about the expulsion of a fertilised ovum, by whatever method and at any moment after fecundation, is to deny life to a human being.

The contrary view receives no support from appeal to medieval theologians like Aquinas, who, knowing nothing of the modern sciences of genetics and embryology, thought that ensoulment happened only at an interval of some weeks following conception. These theologians still regarded killing of the fetus, even before ensoulment, as a grave sin. The sinfulness of the killing of the fetus is taught by the unbroken tradition of the Church from the earliest times, regardless of philosophical discussion on the moment of ensoulment. The Sacred Congregation for the Doctrine of the Faith, in a Declaration on Procured Abortion (November 1974) states: "Throughout the history of the Church, the Fathers of the Church, her pastors, her Doctors, have taught the same doctrines: diversity of opinion regarding the moment of infusion of the spiritual soul never led to any doubt regarding the wrongfulness of abortion" (No. 7). Later on, the Declaration states: "(The fetus) will never become human if it is not human already from that moment (of fecundation). This thesis has always been accepted as true (and its truth is completely independent of debates on the moment of animation)". In a footnote, the Sacred Congregation repeats: "This

Declaration deliberately leaves aside the question of the moment of infusion of the human soul ... Our moral position is independent of this question." It is false to suggest that the morality of expulsion of the fetus in the earliest stages following fertilisation is an open question.

2. TO PARAGRAPH 12
Since the publication of the Pastoral, the campaign of sectarian assassination has gone on claiming new victims and plumbing yet new depths of barbarism. The number of victims now stands at approximately 412.

3. TO PARAGRAPH 89
To say that the *state* of virginity is superior to the married *state* is certainly not to imply that those who have taken a vow of virginity are superior *as persons*, or as Christians, to those in the married state. In fact the contrary may often be true. The Pastoral is talking about the states of life, not about individual persons.

What is stated in this paragraph is simply the teaching of our Lord and the unbroken tradition of the Church. Our Lord said that in heaven the state of marriage will have been transcended and they shall "be like the angels". Christian marriage is in part a reality of this world (though in it Christ elevates the this-worldly values of human love and parental affection and integrates them into the grace-filled reality of his new Covenant); the state of consecrated virginity is in principle an anticipation of the reality of "the next world". To ignore this vital element in the tradition of the Church would be to falsify that tradition.

Here it may be interesting to refer to two Protestant witnesses to the value and meaning of celibacy. Max Thurian of Taizé, in a book called *Mariage et célibat*, writes: "In the prophetic 'parable' of the Church, the state of celibacy announces that in the Kingdom 'they do not marry'; because there is a love which is more total and more absolute than conjugal love" (p. 20). Thurian also quotes Karl Barth as saying: "One thing is certain – and the Protestant ethic has passed it over too lightly in its promotion of marriage as against the Roman discipline of celibacy: Jesus Christ himself, truly human as he was, never had any other love, any other fiancée or spouse, any other family or any other home, apart from his Church" (p. 46). Thurian's work constituted a call to Protestantism for a new appreciation of celibacy.

4. TO PARAGRAPH 112
Nothing in this paragraph implies that everyone who uses artificial methods of contraception is acting from the "contraceptive mentality" as here described. The expression "contraceptive mentality" is used to describe a climate of opinion or a general approach to life which is manifestly widespread in Western society at the present time and which is often referred to as "the permissive society". It is obvious that some people who use artificial contraceptives, while they are doing something that is morally wrong, may at the same time be people who abhor the scale of values of the permissive society. Indeed it is also possible – though undoubtedly less likely – that some people who use natural methods of contraception (see Nos. 113–4) may share the

contraceptive mentality to some degree. Once again, as with the paragraph on virginity, the Pastoral is not here speaking of individual cases.

The term "contraceptive mentality" is a well-known one to describe that climate of moral opinion in the permissive society to the growth of which the widespread use of contraceptives in recent decades has undoubtedly been a major contributing cause. To deny this is to deny a manifest sociological fact. Incidentally the so-called "majority report" of the Papal Commission on the Family as far back as 1967 referred to the contraceptive mentality as "a mentality and way of married life which, in its totality, is egoistically and irrationally opposed to fruitfulness"; and it declared that this contraceptive mentality and practice "has been condemned by the traditional doctrine of the Church and will always be condemned as gravely sinful".

5.   TO PARAGRAPH 127
Pope Paul has recently reminded us of this in his Apostolic Exhortation, *Gaudete in Domino*, "On Christian joy" (9 May 1975).

STUDY GUIDELINES

These notes are not exhaustive; they are merely an indication of possible approaches in getting to know the text of the pastoral.

Part One
YES TO LIFE

PARAGRAPHS 1–8
1. Paragraph 4 explains why human life is so valuable. Does it give you any ideas on the subjects liable to be discussed in the rest of the letter ?
2. The bible is quoted five times in this letter. Examine the value of each quotation.

PARAGRAPHS 9–20
3. Why does the Church teach that abortion is wrong?
4. The state laws of some civilised countries permit abortion. Why doesn't this make it right?
5. Why are the four examples given in paragraph 16 an embarrassment to legal people who support abortion ?

PARAGRAPHS 20–26
6. This section describes the human problems that are used to support the argument for abortion. How does the letter show that while the church has sympathy for the problems she still teaches that abortion is not the answer?

PARAGRAPH 27–30
7. Discuss what the title of Part One (*Yes to Life*) means to you by now.

PARAGRAPHS 31–33
8. Link these paragraphs with paragraph 4 and see how they develop what was said in paragraph 4.
9. A number of human rights are discussed here. Why are they included at this point ?
10. This section is a summary of part of the Church's social teaching. Try to find out more about it.
11. Sometimes a better understanding of one section may be arrived at by studying it in the context of other sections. You might link paragraphs 34–37 with paragraph 70, for example. Paragraphs 38–42 might be linked with paragraphs 107–110.

Part Two
THOU SHALT NOT KILL

12.   A valuable summary of Part One.

PARAGRAPH 48
13.   Like paragraph 4 in Part One this is a key paragraph and ought to be kept in mind in all discussion in Part Two.

PARAGRAPHS 49–54
14.   Before discussing this section there could be a useful debate on the principle: "The end does not justify the means". Then these paragraphs should be read to see how this principle is broken by the people who support euthanasia.
15.   There are a number of references to abortion here. Why?

PARAGRAPHS 55–57: 67–69
16.   We are taken inside the minds of the old and the fatally ill. Study the thoughts and the emotions that are described here and discuss why it is argued that euthanasia is both insensitive and unchristian.

PARAGRAPHS 58–62
17.   Try to get a copy of *The Rite of Anointing and Pastoral Care of the Sick* and the Masses for the Dead from the Roman Missal. Study the beautiful prayers and selections from the scriptures.

PARAGRAPHS 63–66
18.   These are difficult paragraphs. Try to think of examples and situations that might simplify them.

PARAGRAPH 70
19.   Reread paragraphs 34–37. Refresh any discussion you may have had on the principle that "the end does not justify the means". Then see how this principle is used in all the examples given in paragraph 70.

PARAGRAPHS 70–78
20.   At present few Irishmen can discuss violence unemotionally. It is important, therefore, to read this part of the pastoral letter in the light of the principles running through the whole letter. Paragraphs 4, 43, 45–48, 54 could be read along with 71–78.

Part Three:
LOVE IS FOR LIFE

PARAGRAPHS 80–86
21. An understanding of Part Three depends to a great extent on these paragraphs. The ideas discussed are quite difficult, and time should be spent in getting the progression of ideas clear.

PARAGRAPHS 87–88
22. The letter speaks about attitudes that dehumanise sex. Discuss this. Could the society that you live in be said to do this?

PARAGRAPHS 89–92
23. How is celibacy a way of saying Yes to life?

PARAGRAPHS 93–94
24. This section should be linked with paragraphs 40–42.

25. Why does the Church teach that sexual intercourse is fully human only within marriage?

PARAGRAPHS 95–96
26. What does your group think of these ingredients of a happy marriage?

PARAGRAPHS 97–98
27. Marriage – Irish Style. An accurate picture?

PARAGRAPHS 99–100
28. "The joy of sacrificing oneself for the happiness of others." Is this true? Can you find examples in your own experience?

Part Four:
LOVE GIVES LIFE

31. The encyclical *Humanae Vitae* is mentioned often in this letter. Your group might read it at this point. Throughout all of Part Four the letter and the encyclical explain each other.

Paragraphs 107–110
32. Link what is said here with paragraphs 56–57.

Paragraphs 111–112
33. Reread paragraphs 86–88. Why is the contraception mentality a negative one for a Christian?

Paragraphs 113–118
34. Dr. Marshall's book *Preparing for Marriage* is a very useful reference book on Catholic principles on birth regulation.

Paragraphs 119–123
35. Your group should look back in the letter and find reasons why a Christian must be critical of many modern attitudes to sex.

Paragraph 124
36. There is more to this paragraph than the first sentence. Tease out the references to "conscience," "subjective guilt", "God's mercy".
37. Why must a confessor say that contraception is wrong ?

Paragraphs 125–127
38. A beautiful summary of the Christian life. It is interesting to go through the text of the Mass, the Marriage Rite and the Anointing of the Sick and find the same ideas expressed in prayer and scripture.

Daughters of St. Paul

IN MASSACHUSETTS
     50 St. Paul's Avenue, Boston, Ma. 02130
     172 Tremont Street, Boston, Ma. 02111
IN NEW YORK
     78 Fort Place, Staten Island, N.Y. 10301
     59 East 43rd St., New York, N.Y. 10017
     625 East 187th Street, Bronx, N.Y. 10458
     525 Main Street, Buffalo, N.Y. 14203
IN NEW JERSEY
     84 Washington Street, Bloomfield, N.J. 07003
IN CONNECTICUT
     202 Fairfield Avenue, Bridgeport, Ct. 06604
IN OHIO
     2105 Ontario St. (at Prospect Ave.), Cleveland, Oh. 44115
     25 E. Eighth Street, Cincinnati, Oh. 45202
IN PENNSYLVANIA
     1719 Chestnut St., Philadelphia, Pa. 19103
IN FLORIDA
     2700 Biscayne Blvd., Miami, Fl. 33137
IN LOUISIANA
     4403 Veterans Memorial Blvd., Metairie, La. 70002
     1800 South Acadian Thruway, P.O. Box 2028,
       Baton Rouge, La. 70802
IN MISSOURI
     1001 Pine St. (at North 10th), St. Louis, Mo. 63101
IN TEXAS
     114 East Main Plaza, San Antonio, Tx. 78205
IN CALIFORNIA
     1570 Fifth Avenue, San Diego, Ca. 92101
     46 Geary Street, San Francisco, Ca. 94108
IN HAWAII
     1184 Bishop St., Honolulu, Hi. 96813
IN ALASKA
     750 West 5th Avenue, Anchorage, Ak. 99501
IN CANADA
     3022 Dufferin Street, Toronto 395, Ontario, Canada
IN ENGLAND
     57, Kensington Church Street, London W. 8, England
IN AUSTRALIA
     58, Abbotsford Rd., Homebush, N.S.W., Sydney 2140,
       Australia